Godard: Images, Sounds, Politics

D1604436

How does capital function?

A bit like this, perhaps.

Someone poor and a zero	equals	someone less poor.
Someone less poor and again a zero	equals	someone even less poor.
Someone even less poor and again a zero	equals	someone richer.
Someone richer and again a zero	equals	someone even more rich.
Someone even more rich and again a zero	equals	someone even richer again.

Capital functions like that.

At a given moment it adds up, and what it adds up are zeros.
but zeros which represent tens, hundreds, thousands of you(s) and me(s).
so not really zeros after all, the capitalist would say.

We must see, learn to see that when the time comes
to add up all the defeats and victories, very often we have been fucked and
we've been fucked because we, I, didn't want to see, you, she, he, nobody
wanted to see that all their dreams are represented . . . he didn't want to see that
all his dreams are represented at a given moment, given and taken back, by zeros
which multiply them. Yes, but as they're zeros, they multiply and simultaneously
cancel out; and we haven't had the time to see that it's at that moment, at
that place, that our hopes have been reduced to zero.

From Ici et ailleurs

Colin MacCabe

GODARD: IMAGES, SOUNDS, POLITICS.

Text: Colin MacCabe with Mick Eaton and Laura Mulvey
Interviews: Jean-Luc Godard
Advice: Ben Brewster
Film availability: Roma Gibson, Robert Beeson, Pam Engel
Photography: Eric Sargent
Production stills: Anne-Marie Miéville
Production: Geoff Jenkins, Vic Fanthorpe
Tim Fox, Steve Redwood, Angela Martin,
John Winckler, Tina Rowe
Design: Richard Hollis

Indiana University Press
Bloomington

Manufactured in Great Britain

Library of Congress Cataloging in Publication Data

MacCabe, Colin
      Godard; images, sounds, politics.

      Bibliography: p.
      1. Godard, Jean-Luc, 1930 -   I. Godard, Jean-Luc,
      1930 -   II. Title.
      PN1998.A3G6239   791.43'0233'0924   80 -8592
      ISBN 0 - 253 - 12384 - 4
      ISBN 0 - 253 - 21266 - 9 (pbk.) 1 2 3 4 5 84 83 82 81 80

For Fergus and Johanna

Colin MacCabe teaches English language and literature at Cambridge University where he is a Fellow of King's College. He is the author of *James Joyce and the Revolution of the Word* and editor of *The Talking Cure: Essays in Psychoanalysis and Language.*

Laura Mulvey is a film-maker and teacher. Together with Peter Wollen she has made *Penthesilea, Riddles of the Sphinx* and *Amy!*
She teaches at Bulmershe College of Further Education in Reading.

Mick Eaton is a film-teacher based in the East Midlands. He has edited *Anthropology, Reality, Cinema: the Films of Jean Rouch* and is currently working on a film script about Marco Polo.

Over the past ten years all three authors have contributed to the work of the Education Department of the British Film Institute, the Society for Education in Film and Television, and its theoretical journal, *Screen.*

Contents

Interviews with Jean-Luc Godard
appear at the end of each chapter

Note on references and images

The majority of references to books and articles give simply a name and a date. Full bibliographical details appear in the select bibliography.

Almost all the film images in this book are of whole frames as they appear on the screen. In a very few cases production stills have been used, and some of the images from **Numéro deux** show single images from frames which are composed of more than one image.

DEVANT QUI
DOIT-T'ON PARLER
DEVANT CEUX QUI
ETOUFFENT
LE VRAI
QUI PAIE
LES COSTUMES
LE GANGSTER

From **Jean-Luc**

Two or Three Things
I've Heard about Godard

'Well, of course I liked Godard's films before '68 but . . .

From **A bout de souffle**

From **Pierrot le fou**

. . . since he swallowed all that dogmatic Maoism, he just isn't interested in the cinema any more.'

From **Pravda**

'The trouble with film-makers like Godard is that
they're so obsessed with themselves that they don't care about the audience. . .

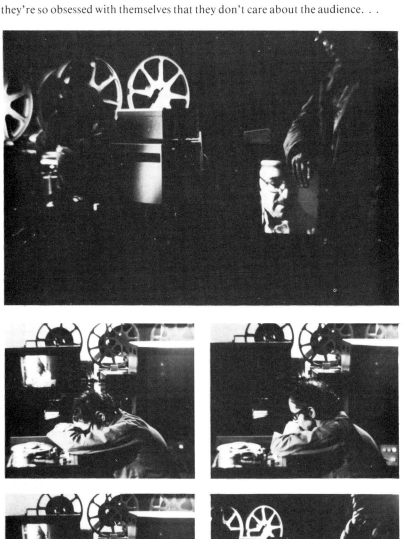

From **Numéro deux**

'. . . When I go to the cinema I want to be entertained.'

Susan George in *The Strange Affair*

Clint Eastwood in *Dirty Harry*

'Godard is the most important film-maker since Eisenstein, sorry I mean Vertov. Only he has clearly posed the problems of politics and art in terms of the consumer society in which we live. He has concerned himself with the representations of our sexuality, the grammar of the advertisements in which we live and . . .

From **Deux ou trois choses**

From **Une Femme mariée**

. . . since 1968, this investigation has simply become more acute, more political. The investigation of advertisements and Hollywood has widened to include every aspect of modern communications.'

Magazine images in **Letter to Jane**

Magazine images in **Photos et Cie**

From **Vent d'est**

'But Godard hasn't made any films in the last ten years, has he?'

NEW REALM Distributors together with the Star Group
say **Thanks a MI££ION!**
to darling
Emmanuelle
...£1,010,000 NET

☆ PRINCE CHARLES AND
NOW AT ☆ scene 4

JAWS 'A'

Now playing at 120 cinemas
in the U.K.

Cinema International Corporation
The sign of a good movie

THE
FRENCH
CONNECTION
SHATTERS
CARLTON
RECORD

ALL-TIME 7-DAY RECORD
("BUTCH CASSIDY AND THE SUNDANCE KID")
BEATEN BY **20%**

Highest ever Tuesday take
Highest ever Wednesday take
Highest ever Thursday take
Highest ever Friday take
Highest ever Saturday take
Highest ever Sunday take
Highest ever Monday take
Highest ever Late Night Show take

The problem is: to get back to zero.

From **Le Gai Savoir**

In 1968, after a decade of influential and prolific film-making, Jean-Luc Godard disappeared from view. ★

A narrative of his disappearance and the variety of film-making practices in which he has since engaged immediately introduces a set of terms that will enable us to understand his films both before and after '68. The manner of his disappearance is instructive because it demonstrates some of the problems that

★ There are details of all Godard's work, both pre- and post-'68, in the check list at the end of the book (pp.169-173). A variety of books have dealt with Godard's early career of which the most notable is Roud (1970). See also the select bibliography, p.174.

Godard felt were posed by the traditional cinema. Godard didn't disappear by fleeing Paris (where he had lived and worked for twenty years) nor by going into hiding. He disappeared by refusing to make films as he had done before. This refusal did not mean that he abandoned film-making; indeed, since 1968 Godard has completed twelve films and eighteen hours of television programmes and is currently at work on three other projects. But if his films existed as material entities, most (though not all) simply didn't exist for the cinema. Without normal production or distribution Godard disappeared, this disappearance demonstrating how films and film-makers have reality only within a very specific set of production relations.

Godard's concern to abandon and question this reality implied an engagement with two aspects of cinema, aspects which seem evidently separate but which Godard analyses as indissolubly linked. On the one hand the financing of films, the methods of production and distribution and, on the other, the organisation of sounds and images which composes the films themselves.

Both these aspects present themselves as so evident, as so natural, that it requires a real effort to understand how Godard was trying to transform them or why he felt that it was so essential to break with them. However, the fact that the production of films is financed through specific forms of national and international distribution, the fact that the audience has no existence for the makers of the film except as an audience which goes to the cinema and pays money and thus has no identity except a commercial one, these features of what might be called the institution of cinema are a major determinant of the organisation of sounds and images in particular films. Crucially this requires a fixed relation of dependence between sound-track and image whether priority is given to the image, as in fiction films (we see the truth and the sound-track must come into line with it) or to the soundtrack, as in documentary (we are told the truth and the image merely confirms it). In both cases what is

From **Le Gai Savoir**.
Still 2: Juliet Berto picking up a mirror.
Still 3: her reflection.

So what is at stake is one's image
of oneself

I said

'image of oneself'

and she said

'Image of nylon'

presupposed is the possibility of direct address to the audience but as the audience is not addressed either as individuals or as members of particular collectivities (family, work, school) they find their place to see and hear only as members of a cinema audience. The only available evidence is that of immediate sight and sound and the film's activity is to make the two coincident. The effect of this coincidence of sound and image is to offer us images of ourselves as men and women, workers and bosses, mothers and fathers but images that address us in the cinema rather than in any other of our activities. This is not to deny that these images have a reality and a force in our existence but to indicate that their production is completely divorced from the everyday business of our lives.

Godard's refusal to continue to make films as he had done before was a much more radical refusal of the cinema than that made by those directors who for political or artistic reasons abominate the distribution system and its control over production. Normally such directors merely demand control of the production process rather than asking what relations are at work in the production process itself as it is evidently understood. In 1968 many French film-makers radicalised by the experience of the strikes and demonstrations wished to find new methods of distribution for the political films that they now wanted to make. Godard refused to see distribution as the major problem because that presupposed that it was evident how one should make political films. It was this more basic question that Godard was to ask and it is summed up in one of the slogans adopted by the Dziga-Vertov group: 'The problem is not to make *political* films but to make films *politically*'.

One of the major differences between Godard and other political film-makers, and one on which he is keen to insist, is that Godard's political concerns grew out of his work on film and were not imported into his film-making. When, in 1959, Godard achieved immediate fame with his first feature film **A bout de souffle (Breathless)**, he was classed as

19

part of the *nouvelle vague*, the generation of young film-makers which included Rivette, Rohmer, Truffaut and Chabrol. His films seemed to share their fascination with Hollywood cinema and what singled him out for the critics was a pessimistic romanticism and a particularly elliptical cutting style rather than specifically political concerns. If, in retrospect, the politics of the image very quickly came to the forefront of Godard's work in the form of an obsession with advertising and the relation between sound and image, critics continued to read Godard in the light of his earliest concerns until in 1966 with **Masculin/Féminin** Godard began a series of explicitly political films which ended with his withdrawal from the traditional cinema.

The necessary link between politics and the image which illuminates the whole of Godard's work but which critics found so difficult to see finds one of its clearest statements in the film that Godard shot for French television before May 1968 but only edited in 1969. Entitled **Le Gai Savoir (Joyful Knowledge)**, the film was proposed as an adaption for television of Jean-Jacques Rousseau's eighteenth-century treatise on education, *Emile*. Rousseau chose to set out his ideas on education by writing a novel about the perfect education of the eponymous child, Emile. The film consists of a series of conversations in a darkened television studio between two characters (played by Jean-Pierre Léaud and Juliet Berto). Although it may seem to have little to do with Rousseau's eighteenth-century novel, in fact it is very close to the spirit of Rousseau's text in that it takes a contemporary form (in Rousseau's case the novel, in Godard's the television programme) to set out the problems of education.

For Godard, and for the characters in the film, the central problem of education is to provide some understanding of the sounds and images that bombard us in our daily lives. Such an understanding must be based on grasping the relation between sound and image because until we grasp that we will not, in the words of **Le Gai Savoir**, be able to make real television

From **Le Gai Savoir**

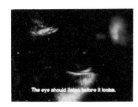

From Le Gai Savoir

or cinema. Instead, all that we can engage in is a repetition of sounds and images in which we are controlled by a language that we do not understand — an ignorance that applies just as much to the makers of television or film as it does to viewers. Just as Rousseau's novel offers an imaginary ideal curriculum, so Godard suggests a three-year course which would enable us to answer the question of who is speaking in any image or articulation of images. The mythical three-year course proposed in **Le Gai Savoir** is not an unreasonable description of Godard's own activity in the three years after 1968. Taking his film at its word: that it was necessary to start from zero; more exactly, as Juliet Berto points out, to *get back* to zero, Godard began an investigation into the language of film which is perhaps the most conscious and most rigorous in the history of the cinema.

The immediate aftermath of May '68 was, however, composed of a series of false starts. After shooting **Le Gai Savoir** and before editing it, Godard had to finish shooting a film with the Rolling Stones which was to appear as **Sympathy for the Devil** (Godard's own version of the film was entitled **One Plus One** and included no final complete version of the song). In the immediacy of the May events he had collaborated in the production of **Cinétracts**, short silent anonymous montages of stills made very quickly for instant distribution, and in August of that year he made **Un Film comme les autres (A Film Like Any Other)** which combined images of May with a soundtrack predominantly composed of conversations between workers and students. Godard then went to America to make a film produced by the American *cinéma-vérité* film-makers, Leacock and Pennebacker. Provisionally entitled **One A.M. (One American Movie)** Godard abandoned this project after disagreements with the producers, whose own attachment to the simple truth of the documentary image was in direct contradiction with Godard's own investigations. Pennebacker subsequently edited the material that Godard had shot and some footage of his own into **One P.M. (One Parallel Movie).** It was only after a further abandoned project in Canada, provisionally entitled **Communications**, that Godard was able to continue the investigations that he had mapped out in **Le Gai Savoir** in a film shot in England and entitled **British Sounds**.

Commissioned by London Weekend and produced by Kestrel Films **British Sounds** was never shown in its entirety on television. As the title suggests the film is concerned with sounds and how sounds can be used against the image of Britain provided by the Union Jack. The film refuses the defining relations of documentary in which the image functions as confirmation of the sound; instead there is a struggle between the two which composes the film. The correct sound, provided by a Maoist analysis of British capitalist society, is kept in tension with a variety of other sounds and a series of images, none of which provides the *correct* image of society but which, in their juxtaposition, provide the material on which the spectator must work. In its emphasis on the soundtrack, in its refusal of the notion of a correct image, in its explicit Maoist politics and in its financing by a television company which then refused to show it, **British Sounds** bears a close resemblance to the next four films that Godard was to make: **Pravda** (1969), on Czechoslovakia; **Vent d'est (Wind from the East)** (1969), a revolutionary 'western' ★ ; **Lotte in Italia (Struggles in Italy)** (1969), on a young woman militant in Italy; and **Vladimir et Rosa** (1970), on the Chicago conspiracy trials. These films were not signed by Godard but by the Dziga-Vertov group.

★ Vent d'est has considerable differences from the other films of this period in that it was largely financed by a rich left-wing sympathiser, in that it included a name actor, Gian Maria Volonte, and in that it concerned itself more directly with the problems of the fiction film. These differences do not amount to enough to consider it separately from the other Dziga-Vertov films.

Ever since making **La Chinoise** in 1967, Godard had been in contact with Maoist militants from the French Union of Young Communists (Marxist-Leninist). On both **British Sounds** and **Pravda** he collaborated with such militants and from **Vent d'est** onwards this collaboration became formalised in the creation of a group which was named after the Soviet film-maker Dziga Vertov and in which Jean-Pierre Gorin was to play the leading role. Dziga Vertov was chosen as a name to indicate a break not only with Hollywood but also with the tradition of Soviet film-making identified with Eisenstein. Eisenstein's decision in 1924 to make a historical film about the battleship *Potemkin* instead of analysing the current class struggle was defined as a decisive moment of defeat in Soviet cinema. Vertov's importance for the group was twofold: on the other hand he continued, much longer than Eisenstein, to insist that the film-maker's prime concern must be the current state of the class struggle; and, on the other, his emphasis on the importance of montage before the shooting coincided better with the group's practice than did notions of montage in Eisenstein's writing.

The culmination of the Dziga-Vertov group's experiments was to be a film entitled **Jusqu'à la victoire (Until Victory)**, on the Palestinian revolution. Material for the film was shot in Jordan in the first half of 1970. The analysis proposed in the film (the success of the Palestinian revolution) was, however, cast in doubt by the events of September 1970, when the Palestinians were crushed by the Jordanian army. This, coupled with an increasing disintegration of the Maoist movement in France, led to the abandonment of both the Dziga-Vertov group and **Jusqu'à la victoire** in favour of a commercial film **Tout va bien**

(**Everything's OK**) directed jointly by Jean-Pierre Gorin and Godard. This project, delayed by a very serious motorbike accident in which Godard was involved, used major stars (Yves Montand and Jane Fonda) to investigate the effects of May 1968 on conceptions of subjectivity and politics in France and thus to pose, from a non-sectarian position (there is no explicit Maoism in the film) the problem of the relation between intellectuals and the revolution. Later in the same year, 1972, Godard and Gorin made a film called **Letter to Jane**, which through the analysis of a photograph of Jane Fonda in Vietnam raised again the difficulties of the intellectual's role in the revolution and partially criticised **Tout va bien** for remaining caught within the dominant forms of cinema.

If there is a time when Godard can be considered to have abandoned film-making, it is not in the aftermath of 1968 but in the period following 1972, when he left Paris and with Anne-Marie Miéville set up a company called Sonimage at Grenoble in the French Alps. Godard's emphasis on production had moved beyond the shooting and editing of the film, the combination of sound (*son*) and image (*image*) which gave his new company its title, to consider every aspect of production. The growth of video technology seemed to offer the possibility of gaining some autonomy at every level of production and Sonimage was set up with considerable stock of video equipment. At this time Godard seems to have considered, at least in interviews, the possibility of alternative distribution. His proposals were not for a network to be run from Paris — one of the emphases of the move to Grenoble was to work against the whole process of economic, political and cultural centralisation — but rather for an alternative notion of distribution which would operate as though Sonimage was a handcraft industry with customers ordering video programmes for particular purposes. This emphasis on small-scale production was one feature of this period, the other being a re-emphasis on the subjective which found expression in the title for the first unfinished Grenoble project, **Moi, je (Me, I)**. In an interview published in *Cinéma Pratique* at that time he stated:

As for me, I've become aware, after fifteen years of cinema, that the real 'political' film that I'd like to end up with would be a film about me which would show to my wife and daughter what I am, in other words a home-movie — home-movies represent the popular base of the cinema.

Quoted in **L'Avant-Scène du Cinéma** no.171-2, p.52

The use of video and the dual emphasis on subjectivity and production are what unites his next projects, all of them realised with Anne-Marie Miéville. The first of these, and in some ways the most programmatic, is **Ici et ailleurs (Here and Elsewhere)**, in which footage from **Jusqu'à la victoire** and images of contemporary France are juxtaposed in an effort to grasp the gap between the Palestinian revolution (elsewhere) and French consumer society (here). It is the *et* (*and*) which links Ici *et* Ailleurs (Here *and* Elsewhere) which is the focus of the film:

what is the relation between our existence here and the struggle there and how does one produce sounds and images which would articulate the two?

In 1975, after completing **Ici et ailleurs**, Godard and Miéville made **Numéro deux (Number Two)**, which analysed the position of women and sexuality in contemporary society. Shot in video and then transferred on to film, **Numéro deux** has a multiple-determined title: on the one hand it refers to its subject matter, woman and anality, but on the other it is dependent on the fact that it was made with the same director, Godard, the same producer, Georges Beauregard, and the same budget as had been used sixteen years earlier to make **A bout de souffle**. After this, Godard and Miéville made a series of programmes for French television, which were broadcast in the summer of 1976, under the title of **Sur et sous la communication (On and Under Communication)**. Each of the six programmes was divided into two fifty-minute sections (whence their other title: **Six Fois deux (Six Times Two)**, the first of these sections analysing some aspect of the image in relation to society and the second consisting of an interview which held in tension the theoretical concerns of the first part and the specific situation of an individual. The final project that Godard completed in Grenoble was, like **Sur et sous la communication**, addressed to the problem of information: its collection and dissemination in contemporary society. The film **Comment ça va ★** analysed the problems of radical journalism with particular reference to the reporting of the Portuguese revolution.

★ This title moves between two different meanings. Understood as a question, it is the conventional greeting 'How are you?', understood as a statement it is the promise of an explanation of some particular movement: 'How it goes'.

If Grenoble was not Paris, it was still too defined by its relation to Paris, by its not being Paris, and thus Godard and Miéville made another move: to Rolle, a small Swiss town between Geneva and Lausanne. It is from Rolle that Godard's most recent projects have originated and while concerns with information persist, such concerns are more and more inflected by an investigation of the constitutive terms of our subjectivity: the family and the opposition between the city and the country, between factory and landscape. Such emphases have displaced the Maoist politics of the Dziga-Vertov films. Politics is not strictly absent in Godard's films since 1972 but it takes the form of a set of questions asking what a politics here (*ici*) in the Western world would be. A constant counterpoint to these questions is Godard's attention to revolutionary movements in the Third World (*ailleurs*) which try to break with Western (or Eastern) patterns of development. Questions of television and cinema are crucial in such a break and Godard, from as early as 1964, has constantly attempted to work in the Third World. Perhaps in no other field are the links between a technology and economic and ideological subjection so evident as they are in film and television. A Third World country's decision to adopt the technology of Western television entails economic dependence on the West for the maintenance and replacement of the technology and an ideological dependence which takes both the direct form of the buying of massive quantities of Western programmes and the more indirect form of the acceptance of the relations between producer and consumer implicit in the Western institution of television. Godard's interest in these problems has taken a more concrete form with the employment of Sonimage as a consultant by the government of Mozambique and his report for the government on his findings was later published in *Cahiers du Cinéma*. In addition he is presently engaged in producing five hours of television for Mozambique entitled **Nord contre sud (North against South)**.

In addition to their work for Mozambique, Godard and Miéville made a further project for French television in 1978: **France/tour/ détour/deux/enfants (France/Tour/Detour/Two/Children)**. The subject matter of these twelve half-hour programmes, which have still not been broadcast at the time of writing, is two children, a boy and a girl, and contemporary France. Each programme interrupts one of the children in the course of their day's activities and these activities are investigated both visually and in the course of a series of interviews by Godard. Some of the terms produced in these preliminary investigations are then further analysed in the rest of the programme. The programmes do not pretend to reveal to us the reality of the child's experience but indicate the opacity of that experience to that most clear of media: television. The opacity of the child's world is used to reflect on the 'clarity' of the adult experience and the ways in which that clarity is dependent on the forms of television. The programmes can thus be considered, as one reading of the title suggests, as a tour of France by the detour of two children.

Most recently, and contemporaneously with the preparation for and writing of this book, Godard has been engaged on two film projects: **The Story**, subtitled **Bugsy**, to be shot in America; and **Sauve qui peut (Everyone for Themselves)** ★ , subtitled **La Vie (Life)**, set in Switzerland. For the moment **Sauve qui peut** has taken priority and after shooting it between September and December 1979 Godard is now engaged in editing the film as this book goes to press. What is significant about these projects is that they are, with the exception of **Tout va bien**, the first films that Godard has made since 1967 (**Weekend**) to employ stars. In that stars are one of the key factors in the traditional economic and aesthetic functioning of the cinema, these films would seem to presuppose a new strategy for Godard, a further re-definition of his film-making practice in terms of the institution of the cinema. The precise forms of this strategy are not predictable but insofar as it depends on his past practice and analysis, two terms will be central to its understanding: money and montage.

★ Godard has since chosen **Slow Motion** as the English title for this film.

★ Note: The interviews with Godard, largely conducted in English, are edited from a conversation taped in Rolle at the Sonimage studios on Saturday 15 December 1979.

I am grateful to Beverley Brown for her help with the transcriptions, to Denis MacShane and Helga and Kiernan Ryan for their hospitality in Geneva and to Anne-Marie Miéville and Jean-Luc Godard for their patience.

Colin MacCabe:

For many people your films come to an end in 1968. But in fact the only time that you would seem not to have made any films is between 1972 and 1974. Can you say something about what you were doing then — in the period after you moved to Grenoble?

Jean-Luc Godard:

Moving. That took a long time and then one began again in '73 with _Ici et ailleurs_. That took a long time, a lot of work — two years. And setting up the studio and moving took a lot of time. Yes, it was mainly _Ici et ailleurs_ and after that we wanted to make two films a year and in fact it's been about one a year.

In the immediate post-'68 period the emphasis was very much on production but in the interviews that you gave around the time that you set up Sonimage in Grenoble it appeared that you envisaged a different kind of distribution: film and video as a handcraft industry.

Yes, but the more we lowered the prices, the less we were offered. And then we turned to television for finance. That was the start of our work for television.

There was also a project for a film entitled **Moi, je.**

Yes, but it was never made.

Could you tell me about it?

It was an analysis of . . . you know, there were a lot of projects, an awful lot of projects that never got done.

26

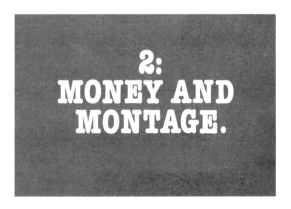

**2:
MONEY AND
MONTAGE.**

If you want to write a book about me then there is one thing you must put in: money.
The cinema is all money but the money figures twice: first you spend all your time
running to get the money to make the film but then in the film the money comes back
again, in the image.

Godard in conversation

Getting your money's worth:

Standing in for the audience:
an actor

Realism:
Genuine US helicopters

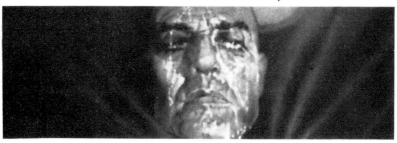

Star:
$2,000,000

Spectacle:
500 smoke bombs
100 phosphorous sticks
1200 gallons of gasoline
35 sticks of dynamite in 50 water explosions
2,000 rockets, flares & traces
5,000 feet of detonating cord

50 Top-Grossing Films

Compiled by Standard Data Corp., N.Y.

(WEEK ENDING JANUARY 17)

TITLE	DISTR	THIS WEEK $	RANK	LAST WEEK $	RANK	CITIES	FIRST RUN	SHOW CASE	SCREENS	AVG PER SCREEN	WEEKS ON CHART	TOTAL TO DATE $
	WB	2,461,556	2	3,424,808	1	20	21	112	133	18,510	5	19,715,6
	COL	1,650,280	3	1,573,805	2	20	25	132	157	10,511	4	9,784
	WB	1,062,290	4	1,013,824	3	19	19	130	143	7,428	4	6,289
SUITE	UA	721,534	5	624,183	7	14		56	75	9,620	4	4,248
CH WAY BUT LOOSE	UA	396,833	6	531,733	15	2		89	95	6,613	10	6,87
OF BODY SNATCHERS	FOX	381,147	7	303,628	2	18	16	63	79	4,012	12	1,2
THE RINGS	PIE	365,177	8	633,571	17	13	12	53	67	4,804	4	7,
(blank)	U	305,215	9	214,466	8	19	14	38	60	3,863	25	25
LDERNESS FAMILY II	U	291,541	10	410,669	19	22	6	67	74	4,164	4	
IZ	PAR	268,126		467,063	12	15	10	40	57	4,001	4	
LAMPOONS ANIMAL HOUSE		262,255	11		10	18	17	50	50	4,370	14	
OF THE GYPSIES								44	45	2,946		
							1		45	2,731	51	2,770
							4	1	45	3,000	21	3,233
								6				6,639

(Continued on page 38)

ut-$5.250) — "Coming Home" ... Voight do ya know,
JA) (2d wk). Voight do ya know, with an extra $5,000 here with $2,940 in three days of second, after $6,058...

Eastside Cinema (UATC) (399; — (Nut-$6,500) — "Brink's Job" (U) (2d wk) (S). Safe bet to do $9,800 in second with $6,664 in three days, after $13,270 first.

Embassy 1 (Guild) (500; $3-$4) — "Late Great Planet (Nut-$11,000) — "Late Great Planet

Guild (Guild) (450; $3.50) "Late Great Planet $6,750) — "Late Great Planet Earth" (Pac.Int.). Not Uranus as pic does $7,513 in first three days, maybe $11,800 for the frame.

Little Carnegie (Reade) (520; $4) "Wifemistress" $6,875 (Nut-$7,450) — "Wifemistress" $6,875 (3d wk) first. Marcello a mellow $5,817 second first day of third after $35,817 second and $32,081 first.

Murray Hill (Rugoff) (568; $4)

This Week's N.Y. Showcases

"Superman" (WB) — Superbowl was kryptonite to pic with $456,347 in three days of sixth in 64 yielding $650,000 or so. Last was $985,815.

"Late Great Planet Earth" (Pac Int.) — Big tv buy coughed up $316,739 in first five days in 65, making $395,000 for lap likely.

"California Suite" (Col) — is palming $350,000 or so based on $254,626 in three days of fifth in 61. Prior weeks would collar $235,000 or so in 67 with $145,000 first. $153,529 in three days of first.

"Circle of Iron" could collar $235,000 or so in 67 with $145,000 first. $153,529 in three days of first.

"King of Gypsies" (Par) — Paramount $200,000 first in 17 sites, Could be $180,000 at 17 sites, in three days, after $57,000 third. Fourth week, $261,148, same in three days. Fourth week, $261,148, same

"Invasion of the Body Snatchers" (UA) — Fourth week in 48. Estimated fifth week indicated by $112,807 in three days. Fourth week in 48. Estimated fifth week indicated by $112,807 in three days.

"Movie Movie" (WB) — Could be $168,000 on first week in 39. Took in $80,527 in pattern. from its $123,752 in three days.

"Magic" (Fox) — Perhaps $95,000 for 11th week in 39. Took in $80,527 in pattern.

"Every Which Way But Loose" (WB) — Estimated at $87,000 or so, fifth five days. Was $203,300 for 10th in 56. Fourth week, $198,185, in 56.

"Up In Smoke" (Par) — In present array of 53 took $85,000 in first day week, 47 sites on $77,831 for five days. Fourth week, $198,185, in 56.

"Bread and Chocolate" (W-N) — Maybe $78,000 in third in 11 with $50,600 in three days, after $90,222 in second.

"Animal House" (U) — Could be $72,000 fifth in 29 with $55,237 in five days, after $129,597 in fourth in 32.

"Lord of the Rings" (UA) — Maybe $62,000 in fifth in eight with $40,000 or days, after $109,702 fourth in 13.

"Days of Heaven" (Par) — Maybe $57,500 in fifth in 13 with $43,000 for so in four days. Last was $65,000.

"Boys From Brazil" (Fox) — Second in 31 a slim $48,193, after $72,479 first in 39.

"The Wiz" (U) — Wuz $30,843 in three days of fifth in seventh in four the lap, after $142,242 fourth in 22.

"Brink's Job" (U) — Falk and knife scrape $35,000 in "Seventh Sea the lap, after $142,242 sixth in ditto.

"Slow Dancing In The Big City" (UA) — Just like in "Seventh Sea with $24,153 in three days, after $44,917 sixth in ditto.

"Paradise Alley" (U) — Or Death Valley with $20,631 in three day here $29,060 first in 28.

"Caravans" (U) — Slow passage; $28,967 in first three days in 33 i third in 14 yielding $29,000 — Slow passage; $28,967 in first three days in 33 i leaving 11 week run at Radio City Music Hall.

Avco I, Hollywood Cin.; Pac) (1,134; 1,5... "Invasion of Body Sn... (5th wk). Slipping... week, $34,370. Also o...

Avco II (Gen... "Movie Movie". Last... so $18,000. Last...

Avco III (Ge... "Same Tim... (5th wk m.o.) week, $20,375.

Bruin, Hol... 668; $4.50) (5th (Par) (5th Last week, case.

Century (Mann) (1... "Magic" (1 wk). Pa... $8,470. Al... Centur... "Ca... Thirsty... Chin... 1,112; ... (6th w... $121,0... Cin... (4,50... Brisl... 1,40... (5tl ... $48...

Amusement Stock Quot[es]

Week Ended Fri. (19)
N.Y. Stock Exchange

12-Month High	Low		Wk's Vol In 100's	Wk's High
43¼	9⅞	Am Bdcst	3600	37
19⅞	9⅞	Ampex	1634	17
16		Avco	3487	25
71¾	15⅝	Bally Mfg.	19241	63
9⅜	3¾	Berkey Photo	307	6⅞
32	16⅝	Blair (John)	150	28
36¾	14	Caesars World	10236	36¼
47¼	37	Cap. Cit. Com.	640	43½
64¾	43¼	CBS	2392	54¼
11⅞	6⅝	Chris-Craft	312	10¼
27½	13¾	Col Pix	2853	23¾
49¼	30½	Comsat	277	43
59¾	32	Cox Bcdst.	281	57¼
47⅜	31½	Disney	2558	44¼
38¾	26½	Dun Brad	1367	34¼
68¼	41¾	Eastman Kdk	8861	63¼
3⅜	2¾	EMI	235	2⅞
13¾	7¾	Faberge	364	9¼
18⅜	8½	Filmways	643	15⅜
45¼	27⅜	Gen. Cinema	167	40
41⅜	19⅛	Gen. Inst.	1494	34
31⅜	22⅛	Gen. Tire	821	26¼
16¼	11	Gulf & West	2841	15
40¼	15⅜	Harrah's	1986	25
15⅜	9	Hwd Johnson	3795	11⅛
28½	13⅞	Litton Ind.	2107	22⅜
55¼	31⅛	Loews Corp.	573	48⅜
45¾	31⅜	MCA Inc.	1054	45
40¼	24⅜	Meredith	170	29
71	32	Metromedia	220	58
54¾	25¼	MGM	1041	46
20⅜	14⅝	Oak Industries	618	20
35¼	22⅝	Ogden Corp.	181	30
33⅝	18½	Outlet	112	24
32¾	6⅝	Playboy	2668	19
17	3¾	Ramada Inns	17395	3
33⅝	23	RCA	3687	2
23½	10½	Republic Corp.	259	1
23	14¾	Rollins Inc.	383	1
16⅜	8¼	S. Juan R.	115	3
35⅜	19⅜	Storer	334	3
25¼	17⅛	Taft Bcdst.	220	3
15⅜	7⅞	Technicolor	216	3
14⅞	7¾	Teleprompter	3170	3
33¾		Time Inc.	1112	3

Diana and Frankie ride thru town. They're going to
join the TV crew that's waiting for them at the
Flamingo or the MGM.

Night begins to fall. Frankie asks Diana about the
book she's starting: " the glamour business". How
it's going? May be the network financing the film
would also be interested in the book ?

Diana asks why it's a european network   that's
doing Frankie's project. He answers evasively. In
spite of his name, he has a lot of problems.

Still driving, Frankie says it'd be a good idea
to start the story in a documentary style, at the
very moment when the evening lights go up, like the
desire in the people's eyes.

People   have been   working all day long for the
industry of day, in factories and offices. Now, they'
re going to work for the industry of night : the
money earned during the day will be spent on the
night of sex, of gambling , and of dreams.

From the script for **The Story**

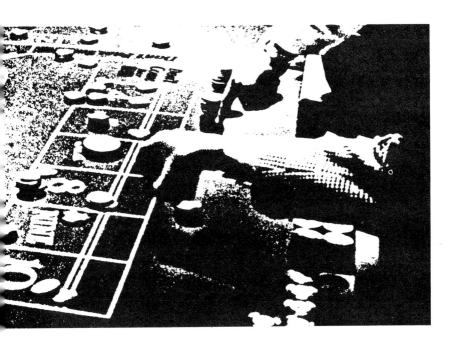

Let the images flow faster than money does .

From the script for **The Story**

Before starting work on **Sauve qui peut**, Godard had spent over six months trying to persuade Robert de Niro and Diane Keaton to star in **The Story**. Difficulties in the negotiations finally decided him to start work first on **Sauve qui peut** but by then he had already written an extensive script of the projected American film. This script is itself a remarkable document, as Godard illustrates the development of the narrative with a montage of photographs, mainly culled from previous Keaton and de Niro films. The 'story' of the title refers to Godard's film itself, to the fictional blind child that Keaton and de Niro have in the film, who is, in some sense, the story of their broken relationship, and, finally, to a film *Bugsy* that a mutual acquaintance of theirs, Frankie, is making. It is their work on Frankie's film that brings Keaton, as a researcher, and de Niro, as a cameraman, together again in Las Vegas after years of separation. The film concentrates on the historical links between organised crime and Hollywood but *Bugsy* will never be made because Frankie dies in a road accident arranged by the Mafia. But we learn a great deal about the projected film and about the character Bugsy Siegel, a legendary Mafia figure who was a friend of Hollywood stars and was engaged in various film-union rackets before being shot to death. At the beginning of Godard's film, Frankie comes to the airport to meet Diane and as they drive into town he talks of his film. He says that

'It'd be a good idea to start the story in a documentary style, at the very moment that the evening lights go up, like the desire in people's eyes. People have been working all day long for the industry of day, in factories and offices. Now they're going to work for the industry of night: the money earned during the day will be spent on the night of sex, of gambling and of dreams.'

The text continues with the cryptic phrase, 'Let the images flow faster than money does'. It is the relation between money and images and the work and desire implicated in that relation which can provide a starting point for an analysis of Godard's films.

Frankie, a film-maker, wants his images to hide their financial determinations, to escape their economic basis so they can function effectively as phantasy. Godard's project is the direct reverse — to slow down the images until the money appears and the phantasy displays its very constitution. And although there can be no question of a simple development — a linear progress towards an ever more comprehensive view — it is undoubtedly the case that the significance of money in Godard's work undergoes a series of transformations. Initially two images of money are opposed — on the one hand there is money in its normal social function where it is understood within a context of work and frustration and, on the other, there is criminal money which functions within a context of desire and liberation. These initial images which were, and still are, current in the commercial cinema were transformed by Godard until they produced a critique of the image itself. The relation between desire and money in the image was connected to the relation between desire and money which is the very condition *of* the image and thus to the position of the spectator. The move from a particular film to the institution of cinema and the question of the political conditions of existence of that institution are traced particularly clearly in Godard's work. The condition of this movement is an obsession with the position of woman in the image which leads inevitably to the question of the economic conditions of existence of these images. Nothing more clearly indicates Godard's later preoccupations than the fact that criminal money in **The Story** does not appear in relation to a particular character's desires but in relation to the institution of cinema: the early financing of Hollywood.

In **A bout de souffle (Breathless)** the narrative development turns around the fact that the money which Michel Poiccard, the character played by Jean-Paul Belmondo, came to Paris to collect and which will allow him to flee to Rome is in the form of a crossed cheque which he cannot cash. This money caught up in a social nexus of financial institutions is

Physical attraction can be an immense source of profit to a woman

From **Vivre sa vie**

opposed to the cash which Belmondo steals from both friends and strangers and which enables him to satisfy his desires without delay, be they to take Patricia (Jean Seberg) out to dinner or to buy himself breakfast. These two types of money set up an opposition between a restrictive social world and one of individual freedom, a series of relations understood within the film as the opposition between normal 'cowardly' (*lâche*) behaviour and abnormal 'normal' behaviour. This opposition is mapped on to sexual difference through the contrast between Patricia's concern with work and a career and Michel's determination to live only for the moment. Patricia's final betrayal of Michel is no surprise to the spectator because Michel has already told us that the attraction of her physical appearance cannot disguise the fact that she is a *lâche*. Woman's attractive appearance hides the reality of her attachment to the social relations which men wish to escape. It is in these terms that one can understand Godard's repeated statement that it is one of his films that he likes least and that he finds it fascist. Its fascism resides in its refusal of the reality of social relations and the propagation of the myth of an existence outside those relations. If **A bout de souffle** represents the criminal as someone who has abolished any restraint on desire, Godard's later films reveal this image as too simple, as indeed an image of money which disregards the money in the image.

Crucial to the connection between money and image is the dislocation of the continuity of looks between spectator and screen. Cinema functions on the articulation of three series of looks, the looks of the characters on the screen, the looks of the camera and the look of the spectator. It is no exaggeration, although there can be other emphases, to say that films produced within what I term the *classic realist* tradition depend on setting up an initial incongruence between these looks, an incongruence which the progress of the film dissolves. In the course of a narrative, one character's view is proved correct, a correctness demonstrated by the camera. It is the

From **A bout de souffle**

From **A bout de souffle**

★ Patricia, it must be said, escapes any final determination by the coincidence of sound and image insofar as the sound, French, always remains incomprehensible to her, an American. Her last line asks the inspector what Michel's dying words meant and this emphasises the extent to which she resists narrative determination. Such considerations may offer a partial explanation for Godard's choice of foreigners for leading female parts in his early films.

From **Une Femme mariée**

spectators' ability to follow this demonstration that assures them of the correctness of their vision. So often in classic realist cinema is the problem in the image, the incongruence of views, caused by a woman, and so often is it resolved by a man that one can characterise classic realism as a constant effort to keep one's eyes on women, to hold them in view. **A bout de souffle**, despite its radical cutting which often 'quotes' action rather than showing it in full, does not deviate fundamentally from this traditional organisation. The problem of the image of Patricia and what she represents, which the film turns around, is solved when we find that she is what Michel has always seen and said she was: *lâche*. ★

In **Une Femme mariée**, which Godard made in 1964, we can notice a different emphasis as the construction of images of women becomes the very focus of attention — and one in which the spectator's look is no longer offered support by a male character. Both the husband and lover of Charlotte Giraud (Macha Méril) are unable to see through her; she lies equally fluently to both but at the same time her own look offers no unifying vision of herself. When we are made privy to her inner thoughts they offer no coherent account of her situation but rather a stream of disconnected phrases. This lack of a coherent view enables the film to break down a unified image of a woman's body, held in a man's look, and to provide instead a series of disconnected images which resist attempts at unification.

35

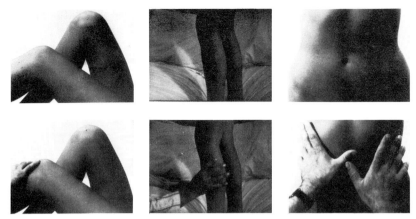

Trying to hang on to the image.
From **Une Femme mariée**

The fact that no dominating male look is produced by the story is what allows the camera to escape that narrative domination which ties it to a logic of point of view and establishing shots.

For example, the camera's movements cannot be rationalised by any reference to the action in the sequence of shots which show Charlotte and her stepson taking a taxi to the aerodrome to meet her husband.

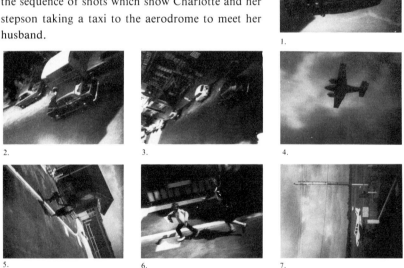

1.

2.

3.

4.

5.

6.

7.

Even more striking is the sequence of advertisements that Charlotte looks at in *Elle,* the women's weekly magazine.

From **Une Femme mariée**

Suddenly we find that the last image is not a magazine advertisement and that Charlotte, whose point of view we had been assuming, abruptly appears in the shot running along the street. Charlotte's look,

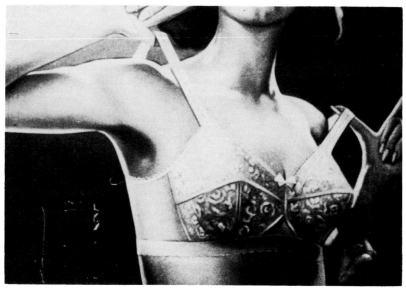

which is the only security that the narrative offers us, is radically insufficient for the task of harmonising the sequence of looks in the cinema; spectators find themselves engaged in an active process of seeing as Charlotte's look refuses to work for them. It is the advertisements that produce Charlotte's look within the film and it is this appearance of images as images in the film which entails that money occupies a different position from that which it occupied in **A bout de souffle.** Charlotte works in an advertising agency and this fact simply emphasises what the film demonstrates throughout: that the problem of the ʝok is inseparable from money. Images and their production are an area of economic activity — where there is a look to be stimulated and satisfied then there is money to be made. ★

★ A film like **Vivre sa vie** occupies a middle position between **A bout de souffle** and **Une Femme mariée.** On the one hand there is an attempt to evade a dominating male look, underlined in the first scene where no character's look motivates the camera position. On the other the image of a criminal money remains and blocks the analysis of the position of women in relation to the image. If the film explores the way in which women are annihilated in a man's look, it holds out, at the end, the promise of a lover in whose look Nana (Anna Karina) can finally bloom before her physical annihilation at the hands of her pimp.

From **Vivre sa vie**

In 1966 Godard made a film entitled **Deux ou trois choses que je sais d'elle (Two or Three Things that I know about her)** in which there is no division between legal and illegal money and in which prostitution is no longer opposed to legal ways of earning money — as it was in **Vivre sa vie (It's my Life)** (1962) — but becomes the exemplary relation to money in our society. The film found its genesis in a newspaper report that housewives in the modern housing estates around Paris engaged in part-time prostitution in order to purchase the consumer durables which were coming on to the market in the wake of the economic boom that France was enjoying under Gaullist rule. The importance of the film is that it abandons all attempts to give classical narrative determination to the protagonist, Juliette Janson (Marina Vlady), who engages in such part-time prostitution. Instead of an attempt to place her in narrative, Godard's own voice on the sound-track poses the question of her position. But the sound-track has none of the dominance over the image that is associated with classic documentary. The opening shots of the film, which present Juliette Janson, make this clear. Whether regarded as fictional or real, Godard cannot identify the colour of her hair and he misdescribes her actions. Insofar as Juliette's position in the film is determined, it is determined by the advertisements that constantly produce images for her. It is the relation between image and spectator, the articulation of the production and distribution of images, that are the focus of the film's investigation and this entails the position of the spectator of the image, be it Godard or the cinemagoer, being immediately posed in the film itself.

Nowhere is this clearer than in the scene in the cafe which alternates shots, from Juliette's point of view, of a woman reading a magazine with shots of the pages of the magazine from the other woman's point of view.

From **Deux ou trois choses**

The normal articulation of point-of-view shots merely relates a look to an object; Godard, by placing one look within another, immediately raises the question of the image and of desire. Godard's comments on this sequence makes this clear:

39

This is how Juliette, at 15.37, saw the pages of that object that, in journalistic language, one calls a magazine (une revue) **being turned over. And here, some 150 images further on, is how another young woman, similar to her** (sa semblable) **saw the same object. Where then is the truth? Full face or in profile? And first of all, what is an object?**

The problem of the object is fundamental to the concerns of **Deux ou trois choses** and a brief reflection will demonstrate how questions about the institution of cinema are immediately posed by a consideration of the object. For, of course, an object does not exist in itself but only in terms of a definite set of relations in which the observing subject figures. Whether I see a bull as so much meat, an element in a landscape or a danger will depend on what I am doing. But this interdependence of subject and object, this relation between world and self, is what is elided in the image which provides the definite relations in which the object appears and thus implies a place to see it from, a place that may have little connection with the spectator. What is important about the predetermination of the image is that it removes the object from the subject's activity in the world to postulate it as a separate entity. What must be emphasised is the reciprocal nature of this relation: that which institutes the object as separate also institutes the subject as self-contained unity instead of divided process. The French word for a magazine, *une revue* (a re-seeing), emphasises how the image determines the position of our look in advance and Godard's selection of a naked woman's body as the image from the magazine stresses how the body and sexuality can be relocated in the image so that sexuality no longer appears in relation to our activities as a whole but only in relation to an ideal viewer separated from any real contact with the object. The primacy of the visual in this process is evident in the scene with Juliette's client from the Métro, where the placing of the mirror so that he can see is the necessary preparation for sex. Juliette's refusal to let him watch her undress plays a complementary role: the act of undressing would introduce process and change where, for the consumer, there must be only position and identity. Godard's activity in the film is to reintroduce the question of being into vision, to restore desire to the eye.

From **Deux ou trois choses**

His earlier themes of the problem of sexual difference and of the alienation endemic to capitalist society are articulated together in the investigation of the stimulation of demand by advertising. It is this stimulation, above all a stimulation of the eye, that produces the subject in pure unity as consumer, the source of an undifferentiated demand whose only relation to the object can be one of possession. This homogenisation is an inevitable result of the economic organisation of society where production is dependent on a demand determined elsewhere. To understand these relations of dependence it is necessary to understand how money functions in the articulation of production and distribution. Godard's analysis of money has one important similarity with Marx's. For Marx money was the condition of certain types of exchange but what was important to understand was that in one particular exchange, that between labourer and employer, what was in question was not an exchange at all but a social relation between those who possessed the means of production and those who did not. This was Marx's distinction between money as money and money as capital. Godard follows Marx in analysing certain exchanges in terms of social relations but there is a great difference in the content of that analysis. Although Godard's film-making practice stresses the primacy of production it does so as the consequence of an economic analysis which emphasises that production is now dependent on ever greater increases in demand and that such an increase necessarily entails an ever greater subjection to the image. Whereas advertising for the economist is simply a means of increasing the number of exchanges in which commodities and money change hands, for Godard it is not a set of money relations but a particular organisation of need, demand and desire in which there is an erasure of the being of the subject in favour of a series of views in which the subject is always centred, in position.

Nowhere is this clearer than in the cinema itself. Films are financed by the raising of money against future distribution receipts. The fact that the film is addressed to an audience which it cannot know except insofar as it goes to the cinema entails that it is only as *viewer* that the audience can be addressed. Immediate consequences for production follow from this fact. The spectator has no particular interest in going to see any particular film because it has not been made for him or her and it is this fact that stimulates repetition — I will go and see again what I have already seen — a repetition that takes two major forms: genres and stars. It is at this point that we can understand why the star system is an essential economic feature of the production of films and why it could be argued that stars have become even more important factors in film production since the collapse of the Hollywood studio system ★. The gossip columns and the celebrity shows in which the stars figure are not unnecessary—they are an essential part of the economic conditions of the cinema's existence. It is true that certain films, *Alien* would be a recent example, do without stars. But these counter-examples merely prove that the star is there as a guarantee of the value of the image and that, in

★ When studio production was dominant, stars were an important economic factor but one largely controlled by the studios. The growth of independent production has transformed the economic function of stars. Whether a film is financed or not often depends on whether a star is willing to appear in it. Maurice →

41

Hatton's *Long Shot* explores some of the economic and cinematic paradoxes which follow from the fact that to get a star you need money but to get money you need a star.

extreme cases, this value can be directly provided by money: one goes to see the special effects in *Alien* because their cost guarantees their value. What these considerations make clear is that the order and content of the images follow the order of money, a sequence made clear at the beginning of **Tout va bien** when two anonymous voices discuss how to make a film, deduce that they need stars and find that to interest the stars they need a story, a narrative. The cost of identity is high when the production of images is determined by distribution and the only way to lower that cost is to change the relations of production and distribution, relations which appear as an evident set of financial constraints, as a problem of money but which are in fact the problem of the control and organisation of sounds and images.

It is when we realise the relation between production and distribution in the cinema, how the order of money determines the order of images, that we can understand why Godard both welcomed the political events of '68 and yet, in contrast to other film-makers, was fiercely hostile to placing problems of distribution before problems of production. It also makes clear why Godard has repeatedly stated that May '68 was not a violent break for him but merely accelerated developments already implicit in his practice. One of the crucial effects of May, however, is that what was implicit in Godard's practice before '68 became explicit under the political and theoretical impact of political struggles in France. Previously intuitive choices were made the focus of a systematic investigation in 1968-71 as production was emphasised over distribution together with a total rejection of the cinematic ideology of vision. If in **Deux ou trois choses** or **Une Femme mariée** the refusal of a view produced by the narrative and an ever greater separation of the various matters of expression are the consequence of an investigation of the situation of women, in **British Sounds**, in **Vent d'est** or in **Pravda** it is the deliberate separation of the various matters of expression in order to comprehend some of the relations between sound and image which composes the film. These concerns necessarily entailed these films being strictly unwatchable by 'the viewing public'; they presuppose an audience united in a set of political and aesthetic concerns and in order to see them it is necessary to share the film-maker's position. Godard's experiments in this period allowed him, however, to formulate more clearly the strategies for breaking with the order imposed by money, or, more exactly, the order which crystallises in a set of money-relations.

The Dziga-Vertov group took its name almost as much in opposition to Eisenstein as in simple commitment to Vertov. Crucial to the group's self-definition was an enlarged conception of montage. Whereas Eisenstein's theoretical writing suggested that montage was an operation limited to the moments of shooting and editing, for Vertov montage was a principle which had primacy in every moment of filming — the Dziga-Vertov group formulated this principle in the slogan: **Montage before shooting, montage during shooting and montage after the shooting.** The constant emphasis of this montage is on separation, on division, on the fact that there is no object constituted outside a practice which simultaneously produces a subject. If many film-makers would take the pro-filmic event as sufficient in itself, Vertov's emphasis is that to constitute this event in self-sufficiency is to impose already a view on it, to produce it for and with its appropriate subject. Montage before shooting entails a commitment to placing before the camera material which is not unified in itself but which already invites contradictory positions from which to see it ★ . Two examples of montage before shooting should make clear what is at stake in this principle. In the *Cahiers du Cinéma* interview about **Tout va bien**, Jean-Pierre Gorin went to some lengths to emphasise how important it had been for them to have unknown and unemployed actors, mainly young, in the role of workers at the Salumi plant where Yves Montand and Jane Fonda are held for twenty-four hours during a

★ This emphasis on the divisions *internal* to the image can find a historical placing in terms of Bazin's praise of deep focus. Godard's originality is to combine this with a division *of the image*. This conjunction was elliptically spelt out in a famous early article on montage that Godard contributed to *Cahiers*.

factory occupation. It might seem that it would have been more logical to have had workers in these roles but, for Gorin, the distance between the workers and superstars like Fonda and Montand would have been too great for the group in front of the camera to be more than a selection of bodies in a situation unified and determined by the script. By employing actors on the economic breadline, relations of envy, jealousy and guilt were established between them and Fonda and Montand which provided some of the raw material of the film in a way that escaped any unification by the script and which, at the same time, would reproduce some of the features of the relations between militant workers and radical intellectuals.

The second example can be taken from the shooting of the film that Godard was making as this text was being written: **Sauve qui peut.** Although there is no script as detailed as for **The Story, Sauve qui peut** shares many of its concerns: the place of the child in a broken relationship, the relations between mother and daughter and the place of work in the production of images. It also, however, contains, as one of its elements, a consideration of the relation between country and city which is not evident in the script of **The Story.** In one of the early scenes from the film, the character played by Nathalie Baye, a photographer who wants to move to the country, goes to meet an old acquaintance who now runs a local newspaper and from whom she hopes to get work. Their meeting takes place in a field where the journalist is photographing a traditional Swiss German peasant game called *Hornuss. Hornuss* pits two sides against each other, each team taking turns to hit a small rubber ball from one end of the field to the other while the opposing side spreads out across the field and tries to arrest the ball in mid-flight with huge bats of wood. Godard had requested the two teams to put on a game of *Hornuss* for his benefit and he had also ascertained the times of the trains which ran across the back of the playing field. The game of *Hornuss,* the meeting between the two characters and the passing trains provided the montage before the shooting: three elements which escape any simple unification into one image.

What the Dziga-Vertov group meant by montage in the shooting became clear as filming began. Godard refused, to the point of arguing at length with the assistant director, to direct the players of *Hornuss* so that the action could be synchronised and a train, an exciting moment of the game and the dialogue would coincide. It was not that Godard did not want all these in the shot but that to direct them would be to lose the advantage of montage, of juxtaposition, in favour of a unity imposed by the director. If the actors could not follow the game as a consequence of their own interest then Godard could not provide that interest for them. In his refusal to tell the actors what to do it might be possible to discern an ideology of truth as spontaneity. Such an ideology, however, assumes a finished and defined representation totally adequate to what is being represented. Godard's activity is in direct contradiction to this: the relations between actors and director are part of the heterogeneous raw material of the film and the director should not act so as to fix the actors in his image. An analysis of montage after the shooting will have to await the finished film but it is certain that the spectator will not be offered an object to look at but an articulation of images to consider. Such articulation always places the spectator's look in question, poses the question of its constitution, makes the institution of cinema the question of every film★.

When Godard introduces the object, which in journalistic language is called a magazine, in **Deux ou trois choses,** the object immediately poses the question of look and position which in traditional cinema it would conceal. It is the introduction of a look where we should find an object, a montage where we attend an image, which reintroduces desire to the eye by subverting its imaginary plenitude. The objects which the image presents to us and to which our only relation can be that of possession necessarily represses our being, our situation in the world. The libidinal investment in the image, an investment on which the economic investment turns, is profoundly narcissistic, an avoidance of the problem of the other. Our acquiescence in this pleasure is bought at the cost of ignoring the conditions of existence of the image, conditions from which we suffer every day. In **Deux ou trois choses** the backgrounds are littered with posters which

Juliette (Marina Vlady) and Marianne (Anne Duperey) pose for a client, versed in the arts of tourism.
From **Deux ou trois choses**

advertise holidays in a variety of exotic places. Each poster places the subject at the centre of the world. No need to confront the question of where his or her look is situated, no need in fact to travel to the place or indeed, even if travel is undertaken, no need to move, no need to undergo the experience of displacement. The world is centred for us by the camera and we are at the centre of a world always in focus. As long as we accept this centring we shall never be able to pose the question of 'who speaks' in the image, never be able to understand the dictation of our place. Godard's devotion to montage, the insistence on the heterogeneity of the visual field, is the only response to a system which decrees that the order of money determines the order of the image.

★ Scenes from the Hornuss sequence and Godard's direction of it appear on pp.161-162.

Colin MacCabe:
                    Is your dislike of **A bout de souffle** due to the fact that it has an image of criminal money which seems to offer a simple liberation from social constraints?

Jean-Luc Godard:
                    No, not really, it's more because it's a picture that I've done for others. A dream of how to make a picture. Perhaps the film should have been made but not by me. It's a picture that's more admired by cinephiles than by ordinary movie-goers and maybe that's because it was a kind of representative of what happened if you took a certain position to its conclusions. I feel that it's not my movie, that there's too much in the picture and only a little bit of it belongs to me. That's why I feel uneasy about it — and why it has taken me almost all the time since to recover myself. I mean you don't make a movie, the movie makes you. It's like work and life, so to recover yourself, to recover at least part of yourself, or what you think of yourself, takes time . . . it means equipment, it means money, it means . . .

45

In films like **Une Femme mariée** or **Deux ou trois choses,** all your emphasis is on the way in which money functions in distribution, the endless stimulation of demand in advertising. And when in '68 you come to emphasise production, it seems to follow from this analysis of distribution rather than from the Marxist analysis of capitalism. Do you think that is a correct description?

I can't say now. I think that we pretended to be Marxists, or that we weren't fully Marxists. It was largely a feeling that we had to debate with ourselves before pretending to distribute goods to the people. We had to produce them in a good way because if not then what would we have to offer?

When we met last year I was fascinated by your saying that the money came back in the image, that all the images of cinema are also images of money.

Maybe I said that. I don't remember what I was getting at. People disagree when their bosses take too much, but they don't disagree when a star takes too much, so it must be that a star represents them in a way. That's why they agree. It's like a king. Sometimes people don't disagree if there's a king and there's a part of them which is in the king. A star in a movie is like that so they don't disagree. Sometimes people like to see pictures which throw away money, James Bond films or Alain Resnais films or whatever. They feel that this is a part of them and they are ready to pay and reimburse the person who's been able to spend and to tell a story. They agree to pay a high price to hear a story or even to hear their own stories. The money enters in a lot of different ways but it's always the same — it's investment, energy, desire, things like that. Sometimes it's money that can be turned into goods and sometimes it's movement.

And what are the ways of interrupting that circuit?

Oh, we interrupt it. At one time I was obliged to interrupt it. I didn't know where I was. It's when one is in difficulties and has no way of speaking about it, it's then that you have to begin all over again. You become an exile. If you are chased out of your country, it becomes a territory in which you can't work any more, so you go elsewhere . . . In a way I've always had a good relationship with and found it easier to get on with producers than directors because at least, and this is the opposite of what is generally said, they are interesting because they are engaged in commerce. OK, so they produce a James Bond movie, it's not very interesting but it's almost more interesting, for me, than Antonioni or whoever because you can at least talk to them about something. For example, the producer wouldn't hesitate to tell you that your film

was bad. He has a real interest in the cinema even if it's only a monetary one. And there's some who've got more. There are producers with whom I've had a good relationship and then there are moments when one's speaking about money and it's a way of speaking about art.

It seems to me that in your earlier films your image for the cinema's economic relation with the spectator was the image of tourism. There's posters and the promise of a movement but never any displacement. Films work like tourism — you're offered a voyage that you don't get — but you try to make sure that there *is* a voyage and the crucial factor in this voyage is montage.

Yes.

In '68 you broke with traditional methods of production and distribution and when you returned with **Tout va bien,** it seemed part of a very conscious strategy. Now in **Sauve qui peut** and **The Story** you seem to be using many more of the traditional economic forms of the cinema, particularly stars. Is this a conscious change of direction?

Perhaps I'm able to see it a bit differently. I don't want to be used by those forms but I want to use them and perhaps use them in a different way. And this raises a lot of difficulties in financing. No, I don't think stars are a change of direction because every time I could use them, I did. Yes, I'd like to use a star but in a way that would not enslave me but help me. I don't want to be obliged to write as though I'm writing an advertisement. Particularly in *The Story*, which is about the 'starry' human system and how the story is the real star, there has to be a star, a big star, for the audience to think of the story as a star lightening our human existence. And that in their story it is the story that is the main star. And you need a star just for the most anecdotal reasons: that it's about Bugsy Siegel and Hollywood. What I've discovered is that it has to be just one star and the star has to play the character I call Frankie. It was a mistake to try to get de Niro and Keaton for the other two roles. Now I want to get Brando to play Frankie and if that happens then all the earlier trouble will turn out to have been a good thing.

In the earlier period you were fascinated with Hollywood and then you rejected it. How do you situate yourself in relation to the history of the cinema now?

I don't know. I feel completely more in it and out of it, out of what is considered the cinema now. I don't know why I see less movies every year. I wish I could see more. I see movie people as complete strangers, as foreigners, people who aren't interesting. But their country is my country.

47

They're almost like oppressors, invaders. That was the sensation I had sometimes when I saw the technicians in the last movie coming near the camera, a camera that I'd bought or hired. Or again some of the things I see in the theatre. I think of myself, yes exactly, like a member of the French Resistance when his country, what he considers his country is run by foreigners.

Is that how you feel about the new Hollywood cinema?

I feel that they're . . . usurpers, yes, that's it. And they are very arrogant. Whenever they say, 'the focus should be such and such', I always want to say: 'What do you know about it? You know and I need your skill but don't say it like that. What makes you think you know about it? Let's discuss it and not shoot right away'. And when you say that everybody disappears.

Isn't there a contradiction in what you've just said. If they're usurpers then there's something they've usurped. So then is there, as it were, an old Hollywood that you still feel is the kingdom?

No. But, after all, at the time they were inventing. I don't know how to say this but people have always had a lot of admiration for gangsters because they invent. Whatever they do they do themselves and that means a lot of work and a lot of invention. There's much more invention in a hold-up by ten people than in a strategic command operation. There's no invention invading Vietnam but Capone had invention. That's why they're admired by people — they are legendary.

Are there any films you've seen in the last ten years that you think are really good?

Nothing. There are long periods when I don't go to the cinema. Then when I do go to the pictures, I go to every one; I was always like that. To give them ten francs against a legend. I'm like everyone — sometimes I prefer to go and see a James Bond picture rather than a Straub picture. It's not as good but . . . I prefer *Gone with the Wind*. But perhaps that's just saying 'in my time, in my time, you know, it was better'. The last picture I saw that I was really glad to see, a good picture and with something new was Marguerite Duras's *Le Camion*. I was really amazed by *Alice Doesn't Live Here Anymore* and some of the Scorsese. That was a discovery. I suppose I could see more pictures but . . . Sometimes I prefer to look at faces or at things in paintings because I can look longer and there are more things to see than in a picture.

3:
POLITICS.

Programme: conceptualise subjectivity in terms of class.

From **Lotte in Italia**

Godard's commitment to a political cinema was signalled in one of his very earliest articles, 'Towards a Political Cinema' (*Godard on Godard,* pp.16-17). Of all the early enigmatic articles it is this one which has proved the most opaque; the English translator commented 'while most of Godard's early articles are fairly cryptic, this one is almost impenetrably so' (*Godard on Godard,* p.245). In fact, however, certain clear terms emerge from Godard's discussion. Talking of a shot from Gerasimov's *The Young Guard* which he claims sums up the whole o Soviet cinema, he writes:

. . . a young girl in front of her door, in interminable silence, tries to suppress the tears which finally burst violently forth, a sudden apparition of life. Here the idea of a shot (doubtless not unconnected with the Soviet economic plans) takes on its real function of sign, indicating something in whose place it appears.

From **La Chinoise**

Godard's insistence that politics in the cinema is a question of signification, the affirmation that the aesthetic and the political are intimately linked, an affirmation aided by the linguistic coincidence, lost in translation, that French has the same word for shot and plan, the emphasis on a moment of emotion as the articulation of the political and the personal — all these can be understood as providing some of the crucial terms for Godard's film-making.

It is not usual to consider **A bout de souffle** a political movie; the conventional wisdom is that Godard does not reflect on politics until **Le Petit Soldat,** and yet the terms of the problems of politics are already assembled in the first film. While Michel and Patricia talk and play in Patricia's room, the radio brings them news of the visit that Eisenhower is paying to Paris and to the recently installed Général de Gaulle. The lovers' international affair thus finds a political analogue. And yet the analogy is formal and empty; the distance from the personal to the political is understood as infinite. Later in the film Michel and Patricia separately descend the Champs Elysées, Michel reading yet another edition of *France Soir* and Patricia trying to evade the policemen who are following her. Their descent is impeded by crowds of people and the policemen controlling them and as the camera pans across from the pavement to the road we see that the politicians' motorcade is ascending the Champs Elysées. In fact we never see the politicians'

50

faces; the motorcade and the police are enough to signal their presence. In the movement of the pan Godard demonstrates the distance between the personal and the political, which is also the distance between the form of the thriller and the form of the documentary. The form of the thriller reduces politics to a momentary lure in the narrative: our only interest in the motorcade is that it explains the presence of so many policemen in terms other than the hunt for Michel. In parallel fashion any newsreel in which the motorcade figures as a central meaning would see Michel and Patricia only as part of the public gathered to observe the two national leaders.

Throughout Godard's early films the search for a form of politics is also the search for a form of cinema which could discuss politics: the thriller again in **Alphaville,** the war movie in **Les Carabiniers.** But as the political pressure of the 1960s grew more intense, and particularly the pressures of the war in Vietnam, Godard's search for a form adequate to the demands of politics which would also constitute a politics adequate to the demands of form became increasingly desperate. No film poses the dilemma more clearly than **Masculin/Féminin.** The protagonist, played by Jean-Pierre Léaud, occupies the position of the oblique stroke in the title caught between the masculine world of party politics in which his Communist friend, played by Michel Debord, moves so comfortably and the feminine world of teenage magazines and pop music inhabited by his pop singer girl friend (Chantal Goya). His own desire somehow to unite and transform these two disparate elements of his experience with the aid of fragments of the traditional discourses of Western culture leaves him without listeners in a solitude emphasised when his only audience is provided by a record-your-own-voice booth. The popular forms of art, despite their appeal, are increasingly shown as ineradicably ruined by their relation between producer and consumer, epitomised in the cinema audience's indifference to the quality of the projection and the idiotic formula questions that Chantal Goya is asked on behalf of her audience by the interviewer for a pop magazine. At the same time there is a liberating novelty in the pop music world completely missing from the habitual politics of the French Communist party, frozen in a repressive stereotype which cannot admit the demands of art or sexuality into the language of politics. For Godard it is not a question of posing the problem of politics in terms of popular art, nor of posing the problem of popular art in terms of politics. In **Masculin/Féminin** and the two films he made concurrently immediately afterwards, **Deux ou trois choses** and **Made in USA,** the problems of politics and art are articulated in the same terms: the terms provided by the forms of cinema.

Godard has never simply accepted the form of the political. So used are we to the daily diet of political information at the international, national or local level that we rarely question the form of politics, the way in which communal decisions are taken and social transformations consciously pursued. It is, of course, the fundamental heritage of the revolutionary tradition that the question of the form of politics is itself political. However, if Leninism was an attempt to hold together this revolutionary truth and the necessity to intervene in the given form of the political, the party being the new form of organisation which allowed of such a double engagement, the historical subjection of Communist parties to the most narrow definition of the political is a testament to the bankruptcy of the Leninist tradition in the developed world. For us in the advanced capitalist countries there is perhaps no instance so evident of the failure to theorise or practically act on the form of the political as the lack of engagement with the new information media that have developed throughout the century. The effects of these media on the form of the political remains, still, largely unchallenged in theory or in practice. One way in which it is possible to view the whole of Godard's work is as such a challenge and a challenge that operates at the level of both theory and practice.

From **Deux ou trois choses**

           Deux ou trois choses hesitates between the forms of fiction and the forms of documentary. Is this a report on the urban transformation of Paris, or the fictional investigation of a woman's life? It is the clash of forms that allows both film-maker and audience to appear as the institution of the cinema becomes an integral part of the film. The 'I' of the title (**Two or Three Things I know about her**) is represented by Godard's own commentary on the soundtrack and the uncertainty of the 'knowledge' is emphasised by the dissociation of sound and image and the increased use of montage. This putting of the devices of cinema in the foreground constantly forces the audience to experience its status as cinema-goers, participating in yet another aspect of the consumer society. The problems of the institution of cinema become the contradictory ground on which Godard can attempt to articulate the terms of the personal and the political and, in hindsight, **Deux ou trois choses** anticipates much of the reflective essays produced by Sonimage.

Before that, however, Godard had chosen to commit himself fully to the political, to that form of politics, Maoism, which promised to revivify the Leninist heritage. This commitment solved, by dissolving, the problems of audience and institution. The film that Godard shot concurrently with **Deux ou trois choses, Made in USA,** provides some of the terms for understanding why, despite the advances of his film-making practice, the cinema was becoming unbearable for Godard. A statement of a more immediate despair, it is dedicated to Nicholas Ray and Samuel Fuller and it marks Godard's final attempt in this period to use the traditional forms of Hollywood cinema. But the political paralysis which provides the content of the film — a publicly defeated left which is further harassed by conspiracies of its own and others' making — is also a paralysis of form. No matter how much ellipsis is used, no matter how often the commentary insists **'we were certainly in a film about politics: Walt Disney plus blood',** the form of the thriller is finally dependent on a specific organisation of image and sound in which politics can only appear as conspiracy, as an appearance the hidden truth of which must be made visible.

From **Made in USA**

And, as has already been argued, this organisation of sounds and images is itself dependent on the specific relation with the audience which is constitutive of the cinema as we know it. **British Sounds** indicated the problem when it announced three years later:

During the projection of an imperialist film the screen sells the voice of the boss to the people. . . During the screening of a militant film the screen is no more than a blackboard offering a concrete analysis of a concrete situation.

It is the relation with the audience that determines the functioning on the screen and it is exactly that relation which Godard broke with in 1968. **British Sounds** makes the point succinctly: **'if a million prints are made of a Marxist-Leninist film it becomes** *Gone with the Wind.'* A film about politics must enjoy a different relation with its audience from that of the commercial cinema; it must be a participant in the reality that it attempts to articulate rather than presenting itself as an observer that can show us the truth of any situation. Insofar as politics is a complex set of struggles ranging from the economic to the ideological, it is impossible simply to represent it to people who, in that very relation, find themselves placed outside those struggles; rather it must address specific audiences in specific situations.

From **Le Gai Savoir**

      To move from the despair of **Made in USA** to the Maoism of **British Sounds** was evidently not a question of some ineluctable personal evolution but the product of a complex of factors involving both national and international politics. In fact Godard was to make three more films under his own name before the formation of the Dziga-Vertov group but it would not be ridiculous to say that Godard was ready for '68 by the end of 1966. Indeed the fact that the next film he made, in 1967, was **La Chinoise,** the story of a group of young Maoists that was uncannily prophetic of the events of the following year, is some indication of that. **Made in USA** is a despairing film which yet allows the possibility of hope. If one fully reckons the left's state of total bankruptcy then at least there is a possibility of starting anew. 'Year Zero of the Left' is a caption that punctuates **Made in USA** and it is from this year zero that one can begin counting again. The despair of **Made in USA** is not a despair of politics and the cinema but a despair of the forms of both, the forms of representation on which they depend, but as such it also marks the start of a radical search for new forms for both politics and cinema. In this total rejection of the existing form of politics, Godard had arrived by his own route at a position similar to that held by Maoists in the West who, following the Sino-Soviet split and the Cultural Revolution in China, were attempting to build political movements that would combat oppression at every point that it was experienced instead of simply challenging this oppression on the given terrain of political debate and struggle. The opening words of **La Chinoise** can perhaps serve as an index of Maoism's appeal to Godard:

On the one hand the French working class will not achieve political unity nor stand on the barricades to obtain a 12 per cent rise in wages, there will not be in the foreseeable future a crisis so dramatic for European capitalism that the mass of workers in order to defend their vital interests will pass to a revolutionary general strike or armed insurrection . . . on the other hand the bourgeoisie will never give up power without fighting and without being forced to by the revolutionary action of the masses. Thus the principal problem of a socialist strategy is, henceforth, to create the subjective

54

**and objective conditions from which a showdown with the bourgeoisie can be
entered into and won.**

The Maoism which Godard portrayed in **La Chinoise**
in 1967 and which was to determine in large measure the films of the Dziga-Vertov
group culminating in the Godard-Gorin movies **Tout va bien** and **Letter to Jane** was
a complex phenomenon. The history of Maoism in China is not yet complete; to
grasp exactly what was at work in the Cultural Revolution, in the ascendancy and
subsequent disgrace of Lin Piao and the Gang of Four, in the current programme of
Four Modernisations, is a task both so difficult and so foreign that for us in Europe it
can only, for the moment, be based on conjecture. However, the history of
European Maoism is easier to grasp. Relatively short-lived, it had ceased to have any
but the most sectarian meaning by the time that in 1974 *La Gauche Prolétarienne*,
arguably the most notable of the French Maoist groupings, dissolved itself. If
Maoism still lives on as a diffuse ideological force, its political significance
disappeared with the failure of the revolutionary movements that found their
inspiration in the French and Italian revolts of the late 1960s and in the protests
against the Vietnam war. The events in China after the death of Mao simply
confirmed this political death as the small political groupings that still sought the
label of Marxist-Leninism tried to reconcile the emphases of the Cultural Revolution
with the slogans of the Four Modernisations.

When the split between Russia and China, nascent in
the late 1950s, became a fact in the early 1960s, almost all other Communist parties
split into a pro-Soviet and a pro-Chinese faction. In Europe there was no case in
which the members of a pro-Chinese faction gained control of the party. Instead
they left or were expelled and founded new Communist parties or movements which
signalled their allegiance to Mao's teaching by the adoption of the qualifying
adjective Marxist-Leninist. This emphasis on the continuity with the founding
fathers of revolutionary politics was one of the distinguishing features of Maoism.
But this theoretical adherence took on political meaning in the immediate cause of
the Sino-Soviet split: the Chinese refusal of the Soviet doctrine of peaceful
coexistence. The Chinese denounced this doctrine as a refusal to face up to the
realities of revolutionary struggle, a refusal which amounted to a new form of
imperialism, social imperialism, in which the Russians connived with the
imperialist super-power, America, to split the world into spheres of influence that
they controlled. This stress on national independence from the super-powers went
together with an aggressive support for the underdeveloped countries, the Third
World, against the developed world and an attack on the forms of aid, both Western
and Eastern, which trapped underdeveloped countries in the position of client
states. This political position was bolstered by further theoretical arguments in
which it was suggested that the fundamental contradiction in the contemporary
world was not that between capital and proletariat but that between the developed

and underdeveloped countries. This thesis found sanction in Lenin's conception of a labour aristocracy, a section of the working class whose dominance in the labour market made it side with the bourgeoisie. Finally, and perhaps most importantly from a European point of view at that time, the Chinese refused to condemn Stalin. The Chinese held that although Stalin had made serious mistakes he could be considered a true revolutionary in that he had refused any thesis of peaceful coexistence with imperialism and had constantly fought against those who had tried to restore capitalism in Russia.

It is this last thesis — that capitalism had been restored in Russia since Stalin's death — which contained the theoretical and ideological potential which was to make European Maoism more than just another communist sect. The Chinese analysis was not based on any classic Marxist analysis of capital in terms of forms of property relations or forms of labour but rather on a moralistic condemnation of the disparities of wealth and authoritarian structures in Russia. It was this, the stress on the importance of personal life-styles in determining the revolutionary potential of a party or country, which was to be the most important feature of Maoism in the West. If workers and militants in Eastern Europe were dissatisfied with the life-styles of their political rulers, they had little option but to live with their dissatisfaction, but in Western countries communist militants could express their distrust of the bourgeois life-styles of their leaders by setting up Marxist-Leninist parties that would break with bourgeois forms at every level.

The stress on the personal, on the daily struggle between the bourgeois and proletarian line in one's own life, was both Maoism's strength and its weakness. On the one hand it really did subvert the form of the political, including within its sphere every aspect of life. On the other it threatened to reduce all those other aspects to the political. This has been the dilemma of Leninist politics throughout the century. The attempt to subvert the form of the political has often resulted in an ever greater dominance of the political. In Maoism this ambiguity crystallised round the figure of Mao himself. If the thought of Mao Tse-tung emphasised contradiction as a principle running through every form of practice, one figure, Mao himself, remained outside contradiction, offering a final resolution.

Mao's attempt to revivify Leninist politics drew on two Leninist ideas. The first was the notion of self-criticism. This practice, which has a particularly barbarous history in the Communist movement, can be theoretically understood in a more favourable light as an attempt to break with certain notions of personal identity and to allow the individual to understand himself or herself as a series of contradictions rather than a fixed essence. In fact, all too often, the practice became a complete subordination of the individual to a political identity which allowed of no contradiction whatever, but there can be little doubt that the practice was potentially an important one and it was eagerly adopted by European Maoists as an important method of breaking with bourgeois notions of identity and politics. Self-criticism was not, however, the key Maoist concept. That place was reserved for the second Leninist idea drawn on by Mao — cultural revolution, a theory not promulgated until some years after the original Sino-Soviet split. This concept had been advanced by Lenin towards the end of his life to cope with the problem that the political seizure of the state and the economic reorganisation of the means of production were not enough to abolish classes or class struggle. It could be argued that this contradiction in fact spelt the death of Leninism, of that particular attempt to theorise political and economic struggle. Be that as it may, Lenin attempted to deal with the problem by talking of the necessity for a cultural revolution which would wrest ideological power from the bourgeoisie. It was never really more than a suggestion and its consequences were never properly explored.

When, however, Mao Tse-tung found himself in the same dilemma in China, with a growing hierarchisation of the administrative and political structures threatening to reintroduce forms of privilege and discrimination which had been associated with capitalism, he used the concept of cultural revolution to engage the Chinese people in a new political struggle, one designed to combat this new hierarchisation. The Cultural Revolution stressed the importance of ideas and of understanding every activity in terms of class struggle but if ideological struggle became the major political task the specific role of the intellectual disappeared. It was an essential tenet of the Cultural Revolution that it should combat the division between mental and manual labour, on which the very category of intellectual depends, in order that the masses could participate directly in the ideological struggle.

This schematic analysis of Maoism should indicate how it was this strand of revolutionary activism that focused many of Godard's preoccupations rather than Trotskyism, anarchism or any other of the diverse political tendencies that participated in '68. It was the linking of the importance of personal struggle, particularly in the ideological field, with a commitment to the Third World that made Maoism an appropriate form for the expression of hatred of consumer society and its basis in underdevelopment elsewhere. Maoism did not dictate in advance the form of films that must be made; indeed Maoism insisted that this was an open question which, as in other areas of ideological struggle, must be solved by a combination of practical experiment and theoretical reflection. The importance granted to theoretical work allowed Godard the opportunity to elaborate systematically the cinematic implications of many of his earlier intuitive choices.

To pose Maoism in terms of its various intellectual components illuminates Godard's relation to it but also poses that relation in curiously formal terms. It ignores the extent to which in the immediate aftermath of '68 the decision to participate actively in a movement dedicated to the overthrow of the existing system of oppression was not an intellectual choice, but rather a commitment to engage oneself in totally new methods of work. If Godard's commitment to Maoism was to wane after 1972, his break with traditional methods of work remained permanent. Perhaps the most important new element was the decision to work collaboratively. The Dziga-Vertov group was always more than the mere fiction that it was often taken for. On **British Sounds** and **Pravda** Godard worked with Jean-Henri Roger and they were joined on **Pravda** by Paul Burron. But the decisive collaboration was to be with Jean-Pierre Gorin, another of the young Maoists with whom Godard had first come into contact while making **La Chinoise**. It was with Gorin that Godard made the last four Dziga-Vertov films — **Vent d'est, Lotte in Italia, Vladimir et Rosa** and the unfinished **Jusqu'à la victoire** — before, under their own names, they released **Tout va bien** and **Letter to Jane**. Godard has insisted, both at the time and subsequently, that his contribution to these films was largely technical, 80 per cent of the ideas coming from Gorin. The importance of this assertion is that it confirms that the collaborative work undertaken with Gorin was exactly that. It must not serve as an encouragement to divide the films into different sections to some of which we attach the name Godard, and to others Gorin, because Godard also insists that, whatever the original provenance of the ideas, the finished films were the complete responsibility of both collaborators. If the technological and financial organisation of the cinema imposes collective work as the condition of the production of a film, the dominant ideology of the individual (be it in that form which privileges the 'creative artist', the director or actors, or in the complementary form which insists on the sharp delimitation of the 'professional competence' of the various technicians) often works against developing the collectivity that is instituted by the very decision to make a film. Although Godard ceased to work with Gorin when he moved to Grenoble and set up Sonimage, Sonimage was anything but a return to an individual method of work. Over and above the collaboration with Miéville which provides the basis for Sonimage's work, each project, be it film or television, is undertaken as a collective enterprise in which every member of the production unit is expected to participate actively.

The distinguishing feature of the Dziga-Vertov films is not therefore their collective production, which continued after the group's demise, but rather the political conditions which allowed the films to be made with a totally different relation to the audience from that implied by the traditional commercial organisation of production. The political situation in France in the immediate aftermath of '68 was such that there was a real audience, however small, for films which were **'no more than a blackboard offering a concrete analysis of a concrete situation'**. If all that unifies the traditional cinema audience is a willingness to surrender a certain sum of money, it is this financial unity which determines the necessity for sound and vision to coincide, for our eye to be confirmed in its ability to see. The Dziga-Vertov films, however, were made for an audience unified in its acceptance of a Maoist analysis of revolutionary struggle. It is this different form of address which allows the synchronisation of sound and vision to be radically disturbed. If the audience accepts the correct sound that can be provided by a Maoist analysis, the question of the images that should accompany this sound is left open — the very problem that the films explore. It is this situation which provides both the interest and the final limitations of these militant films. On the one hand the subversion of the dominance of the image allows the investigation of the relation between sound and image which **Le Gai Savoir** claimed as a necessary preliminary to any real television or cinema. On the other hand the assumption of a correct sound-track implied the possibility of a correct image to accompany it. The advance is that the audience is included in the relation of correctness. There is no question of producing on the screen a correct alignment of sound and image. What is considered possible is that in a particular situation and for a particular audience it is possible to produce correct sounds and images. Hence the fact that to make a million prints of a Marxist-Leninist film is to transform it into *Gone with the Wind*. The problem is that the notion of a correct relation between sound and image is understood in exclusively political terms. The political constitution of the audience produces a dominance of politics where before one had the dominance of the alignment of sound and vision. In fact the Dziga-Vertov films work in that constitutive contradiction which provided both the strengths and weaknesses of the original Leninist impulse and its Maoist revival. The strength comes from the determination to challenge the form of the political by including within it a variety of other practices. The complementary weakness is that finally all these other practices are exhaustively defined in terms of the political.

From **British Sounds**

Both **British Sounds** and **Pravda** investigate the form of the documentary, posing the question of what it is to represent the political situation in a country, be it capitalist Britain or socialist Czechoslovakia. Although both films work resolutely against that traditional form of the documentary which simply produces images which accompany and prove the truth of the sound-track and although the content of the sound-track is contradictory in places, the films persistently pose the existence of a correct sound and a new relation between sound and image which would produce the correct image to accompany it. This final goal of both films is evident in the similar closing sequences in which revolutionary songs accompany the image of a red flag. ★

★ For further analysis of **British Sounds** and **Pravda** see chapter 4, pp.85-87, and chapter 5, pp.114-119, respectively.

Vent d'est, the first film on which Gorin was the major collaborator, is significantly different in that it attempts to deal with the problem of fiction. This immediately poses the question of vision more acutely because there is no place in a fiction film for a correct sound except insofar as it is congruent with the narrative, a narrative which is guaranteed by the fact that we see it unroll. In fact the most immediately striking feature of the film is the refusal to provide images which articulate a narrative. As characters wander across the screen it is the sound-track or written captions which determine their identities, motives and actions. A typical example of this dominance of the sound-track comes in the second section of the film, which has been introduced by the caption 'THE DELEGATE'. One of the scenes in this section is of an idyllic country setting in which one of the female characters is being courteously attended to by a male figure, already identified for us as the union delegate. The second female voice, which has been declared to be the voice of truth, comments:

The union delegate is talking to a lady with a parasol. She is barely discernible in black and white but even in colour her features remain indistinct.

This woman is called Suzanne Monet, wife of the famous painter Claude Monet. In 1903 she published an open letter in *Le Figaro* **to the President of the French Republic, protesting against the striking railwaymen who had forbidden her husband to enter the Gare St Lazare to finish his painting.**

1925: this woman is called Scarlett Faulkner from Louisville (Alabama). A known nymphomaniac, she accused Richard Leverall, Dick Clever and Eddie, a farmhand, of having raped her several times. The local chapter of the Ku-Klux-Klan immediately carried out the execution of the horrible criminals Leverall, Clever and Eddie.

In 1936 this woman has become Ines Mussolini, married to the Spanish representative of the Schneider-Krupp group. She welcomed Franco's troops into Barcelona after they had taken Barcelona from the anarchists and the workers' councils.

From **Vent d'est**

VENTO
LE VENT
D'EST
DELL' EST

'What is to be done'

From **Vent d'est**

In 1969 she is called Rachel Darnev, graduated in chemical analysis from the Vise Farben University in Nuremburg. She specialises in the napalming of Palestinian farmers in the Nablus and Gaza area who refuse to leave their land.

Vent d'est found its original inspiration in an idea of Daniel Cohn-Bendit, the student leader from Nanterre, to make a left-wing western in which a mining strike would provide the central element of the plot. The Dziga-Vertov group argued that it was wrong to think that one could make a left-wing western. Insofar as the film would preserve the same relationship with the audience as traditional Hollywood cinema, it little mattered what the content of the film would be. What was necessary was the disruption of the traditional organisation of Hollywood cinema so as to investigate how images found their meaning within specific articulations determined by ideological and political struggles *and* to engage the film viewer in that investigation. Only through such an engagement could there be a possibility of making a political film. If the film chose to represent political struggle unproblematically without engaging the viewer in the construction of meaning, then the spectators would learn nothing about their specific situation; indeed, insofar as they accepted unproblematically the images and identifications of the film they would lose their capacity to act in a revolutionary manner, for such action depends on attention to the concrete situation which the Hollywood film could only ignore. The political content of a film could not be defined outside a form which engages the viewer in the analysis of meaning and signification — the problem of determining the correct revolutionary line. The articulation of form and content is evident in the introductory section of the film when the sound-track is first occupied by voices retelling all that is left of Cohn-Bendit's plot (later a voice complains that **'They've excluded all the characters who were to have been seen in the film'**) followed by a voice that analyses

61

the history of the cinema in political terms. It is the account of a strike, now generalised to cover any strike, and the problems of how to find images for it that compose the film. To understand the meaning of a strike and to understand the meaning of an image become the same thing.

Nowhere is this interweaving of these two concerns more evident than in the fourth element into which the strike is analysed: the mass meeting (generally and rather misleadingly translated into a literal equivalent for the French: the general assembly). The original impetus for the strike and the role of the active minorities and the delegate have already been investigated and the problem now is to understand the next stage of the strike as the workers gather for a mass meeting. This section is mainly composed of images of the film company lying around and discussing the question of whether an image of Stalin should be used in the film. This discussion is punctuated in the finished film with a variety of images of Stalin. The sound-track is composed of fragments of what the participants in the debate are saying and a voice-over analysis pronounced by the second female voice, which we already know to be the voice of truth. It is this voice that tells us that just as mass meetings can be understood only in terms of the specific circumstances — who are they for and who are they against? — we can understand images only if we ask the same questions. Thus the image of Stalin is used by capitalists as an image of repression but from a revolutionary point of view it is a repressive image insofar as it prevents the proper analysis of Stalin as a political phenomenon. The voice-over insists on the Maoist assumption that when one has analysed the specific nature of a struggle or an image it will find its place in the determining struggle of the moment: the struggle of imperialism and revisionism against revolution.

Just as the section on the mass meeting repeats, with variations, the image of Stalin, so, throughout the film, as in the other Dziga-Vertov movies, there is a constant repetition of earlier images

This is not a just image, it's just an image.

1 — The Strike
2 — The Shop Steward

1 — The Strike
2 — The Shop Steward
3 — The Active Minorities

From **Vent d'est**

Images of Stalin.
From **Vent d'est**

indicating how they have changed in meaning as the film progresses. The aim is the complete evacuation of the meaning of the image into the struggles that surround it, struggles all finally determined by the class struggle. Although the film constantly emphasises the importance of the specific analyses of the cinema, the overwhelming dominance of the determining political analysis leaves no possibility of grasping the effectivity of the cinema except in terms of its function as a liar on behalf of imperialism and revisionism, the complementary world of Nixon-Paramount and Brezhnev-Mosfilm. If **Vent d'est** addresses the audience in a different place from the commercial cinema, that change of place is not effected by the film but by the political context which provides an audience in a place other than the cinema. If the synchronisation of sound and image so vital to the commercial cinema has been abandoned, it has been abandoned in favour of the dominance of one particular element on the sound-track which unifies all the subversions of the traditional relations between image and sound. It is this absolute dominance of the political that leaves the film so oddly formalistic. All the work on the image finds its determination in politics rather than in terms of a series of specific relations between the cinema and politics.

Lotte in Italia, the next film that Godard and Gorin made, while finally retaining the dominance of the political, interrogates the terms of politics much more thoroughly than the preceding film. It is the most interesting of the Dziga-Vertov films and it is therefore particularly unfortunate that it has never been shown in Britain or the United States. Like the other films its title is both misleading and accurate. Whereas we might anticipate endless footage of battling workers and students, we see instead images of one young woman and these images are repeated through the four sections of the film. The aim of this repetition is to investigate the very notion of struggle, to understand the terms of political struggle across a struggle between sound and image. The first section produces a series of images of a young woman militant, engaged in political activity, buying clothes, with her family, with her boyfriend, in her university. This very description is inadequate insofar as it ignores the fact that the images presented are images of one element of each of these activities; there is no pretence that we can *see* her in any of these situations. Rather, a small detail indicates a larger pattern of relationships, the larger pattern being that which the combination of sound and image attempts to analyse. For example, a shot of a spoon scooping soup out of a bowl is accompanied by a voice-over which informs us that she is with her family. In the second section the girl comments on these images and produces new ones designed to show that the first series were only reflections which failed to grasp the reality of her life as a revolutionary. The third section reruns the images that we have already seen while a voice-over attempts to understand the reality of the reflections that composed the first section and thus to criticise and transform the protagonist's account of the reality of her life in the second part. The aim of this third section is to demonstrate the importance of ideology, how our imaginary understanding of our real conditions of existence is the site of a constant battle, the outcome of which has an effect on those real conditions. Insofar as the protagonist ignores the importance of her relations with her family and in the university, she fails to combat bourgeois ideology on its own terrain. Political struggle cannot be understood in terms of simple militant activities but must be widened to embrace every practice. The importance of ideology is made evident in the progress of the film itself. We can never *see* reality because reality is visible only in terms of the forms of explanation available to us. The images of the film constantly change their meaning in terms of the contradictory sounds that accompany them. The fourth and final section of the film has the militant correcting the errors of the second section, which ignored much of her life and overemphasised the importance of militant political struggle. At the end she resolves to introduce the class struggle into every

From **Lotte in Italia**

64

area of her life, to understand 'all the ideological bases of which I am made'. Her political programme is widened so as to conceptualise subjectivity in terms of class.

Although this programme is implicit in Maoism, the formulations of the film are taken directly from the work of the French communist Louis Althusser. Althusser is most probably the leading Western Marxist to have developed the ideas of Mao Tse-tung. Perhaps the most significant of his contributions is an essay called 'Ideology and Ideological State Apparatuses' (Althusser, 1971), which was published in France in April 1970 but which Gorin had discussed with him before making **Lotte in Italia.** Although Mao stressed the importance of cultural struggle, this importance was not theoretically developed and frequently presented itself as a simple Manichaism which divided the world into good and bad, capitalist-roaders, imperialists and revisionists on the one hand and revolutionaries on the other. Althusser eschewed this moralistic divide and developed Mao's insights in terms of an analysis of any mode of production into three instances, or levels — the economic, the political and the ideological — and his 1970 essay was an attempt to theorise the functioning of the ideological instance. Althusser's essay had two parts. The first combated any notion of ideology as false consciousness from which we could be liberated — we all live within systems of representations which never simply correspond to the real. There is no moment of transparency which will bring revolutionary struggle to an end as the world becomes evidently visible. It is not a question of opposing truth to ideology but of analysing particular ideological struggles — the function of any particular system of representations. These systems of representations are not simply a matter of ideas but of particular practices which produce them. The second part of the essay was devoted to a consideration of how those practices were organised on a political basis which had to be recognised and struggled against. The concept that Althusser advanced to describe this political organisation was that of 'Ideological State Apparatus'. Classical Marxist-Leninist theory analyses the state in terms of its control by a specific class and it was traditional to consider that the state possessed a number of repressive apparatuses (the police, the army and so on) designed to maintain this control of the dominant class. Althusser's originality was to postulate Ideological State Apparatuses which maintained the dominance of the ruling class through non-coercive means by producing subjects willing to reproduce the relations of production. Althusser claimed that the two most important Ideological State Apparatuses were education and the family. Althusser's formulations are of the utmost importance insofar as they stress the necessity of ideological struggle across a whole series of institutions but they run into the same contradictions which we have already encountered in our brief discussions of Mao and Lenin. The attempt to transform the concept of the

65

political to embrace a range of social practices is also an attempt to reduce those practices to the political. Althusser's formulation of the 'relative autonomy' of the ideological reveals this contradiction in its very wording. 'Relative autonomy' is an oxymoron: either the ideological is autonomous and then the struggles on its terrain are not to be explained or justified in terms of politics, or it is not autonomous and then it is exhaustively explained by a consideration of the reality of political struggle.

This theoretical difficulty which we have traced across the work of the Dziga-Vertov group took on a practical form with the decline of Maoism in France and the defeat of the Palestinian revolution in Jordan. If the Dziga-Vertov group found a political justification for its ideological struggle in the political audience which it addressed in its films, that audience was in the process of dissolving. Either they reconstituted a political audience or the struggle on the ideological front of cinema lost any straightforward political justification. The immediate response was to attempt to reconstitute that audience in two different ways: first of all through the capitalist cinema (with the production of **Tout va bien),** and then (with **Letter to Jane)** with a new form of film which addresses a new audience, neither the political audience of the Dziga-Vertov films nor the commercial audience of the capitalist cinema.

These efforts, however, were not to be realised until 1972. In the meantime Godard and Gorin shot the footage for the then-to-be-abandoned **Jusqu' à la victoire** and they also made **Vladimir et Rosa** to pay for the Palestinian film. Although work on **Tout va bien** was to have started after this, it was long delayed while Godard recovered from his serious motorbike crash. **Vladimir et Rosa,** the last completed Dziga Vertov film, is by far the weakest. Whether this is because the primary reason for its production was financial, because the group's *raison d'être* was already dissolving or because American politics were particularly resistant to Maoist analysis is not clear, but the stylised representation of the Chicago conspiracy trial intercut with shots of Godard and Gorin talking on a tennis court while other people play around them neither advances the investigation of the relations between images and sounds nor produces an analysis of politics which develops the positions in **Lotte in Italia.**

Tout va bien, however, does develop the positions of **Lotte in Italia,** but for a different audience. If **Lotte in Italia** examined theoretically, and from the position of a militant, the necessity of understanding subjectivity in terms of class, demonstrating that necessity across an investigation of the relation between sound and image, **Tout va bien** attempts to prove this necessity to a non-militant audience, this proof requiring a different approach to the problem of sound and image. If Godard and Gorin

From **Tout va bien**

always claimed that they were willing in principle to make a commercial movie, it is difficult to believe that the practical decision actually to make one was not the product of the political situation which deprived them of a militant audience. **Tout va bien** is both similar to and different from the Dziga-Vertov films that preceded it — similar in that it grants primacy to politics, different in that this primacy of politics is not assumed as the very starting point of the film, but rather the film attempts to demonstrate it. Most significantly, the decision to work in the cinema necessitates a more specific work on that institution. It is no longer a question of producing correct images for a correct sound, that sound being the guarantee of the political audience to watch the film; it is a question of working on the articulation of sound and image provided by the institution of the cinema in order to persuade the audience of the centrality of politics to their lives.

The decision to work in the commercial cinema requires the use of both stars and narrative. An imaginary dialogue at the opening of the film sketches the institutional logic that determines the progress from the desire to make a film to the need for stars in order to finance it and thus the necessity of a narrative to interest the stars. The story itself starts with the arrival of Jane Fonda and Yves Montand at a food-processing factory which has been occupied by its workers. Fonda, a journalist, has arranged to interview the managing director and Montand, taking a break from his job as a director of advertising films, decides to accompany her. When they arrive at the factory they find that a lightning strike has turned into a full-scale occupation and the workers incarcerate them with the managing director, who has already been imprisoned in his office. The events in the factory, involving management, unions and workers, occupy the first section of the film, the second section examines the effects of the events at the factory on the lives of Fonda and Montand and the third section attempts to generalise the lessons of the film for contemporary France.

Jane Fonda recording
one of her weekly broadcasts
to America.

From **Tout va bien**

67

The film avoids any explicit sectarian line in its content. However, Maoism is still the defining theoretical and ideological position from which the film is made and the film's lesson is a Maoist one: that we should learn how the class struggle functions in every aspect of our lives. We must learn, as the film puts it in its final moments, to think ourselves historically (*se penser historiquement*). If the film uses narrative and stars, it resolutely refuses that use of the camera which articulates the looks of spectator, camera and character in order to produce a vision which is also, and automatically, knowledge. Nowhere in the film are there examples of alterations in perspective achieved by moving the camera on its axis, as in the pan, or by means of the lenses, as in the zoom. When the spectator's point of view alters, it is when the camera itself moves in a travelling shot. That knitting together of narrative and vision, whereby without altering its position the camera can effortlessly follow and focus on significant elements in the image, disappears.

But the rupture between vision and knowledge is made even more evident in the lack of point-of-view or shot/reverse shots. It is difficult to define either of these terms with absolute technical precision as they are never the simple organisation of camera positions independent of specific narrative developments. Crudely, however, a point-of-view shot can be defined as a shot of a character or characters looking, followed by a shot of an object or person which is thus assumed to be in the visual field of the character(s) concerned, this assumption often being confirmed by a third shot which repeats the first. A shot/reverse shot sequence can similarly be defined as one shot followed by a second (reverse) shot which includes the space of the first shot. Classic examples of this articulation are a battle-field scene in which a shot from one advancing army is immediately followed by a shot from the position of the opposing army, or a shot of one character engaged in conversation followed by a shot, from the first character's point of view, of the other speaker engaged in the dialogue. Point-of-view and shot/reverse shots not only construct a space that is exhaustively comprehended by the camera but they also constantly offer us the possibility of identification with a character's point of view.

From his earliest films, Godard's use of these techniques had often worked against the dominant conventions. In particular, he rarely used

Example of a point-of-view shot sequence — Glenn Ford looks across a bar at the commotion caused by Lee Marvin in Fritz Lang's *The Big Heat*.

Example of a shot/reverse shot sequence — Edith Evanson offers information to Glenn Ford in the same film.

shot/reverse shot sequences to construct conversations. However, **Tout va bien** is much more rigorous than any of the pre-'68 films in its disruption of the identification between spectator and camera, that congruence of looks which then further enables the adoption of a point of view within the narrative. **Tout va bien**'s insistence on the discontinuity between these two looks makes any identification with one character's *correct* point of view extremely problematic.

It is this difficulty of understanding, this problem of identification, which is both form and content in **Tout va bien.** The first section explicitly deals with Fonda's and Montand's incomprehension of what is happening in the factory. To see is not to understand. The striker who silently paints the walls blue makes the point succinctly. The paintings on the walls which he obliterates are representations of the factory but they tell us nothing. To move inside the factory is no guarantee of knowledge. The manager, the union representative and the strikers all present very different interpretations of what has happened and it is important that there is no action which would visibly reveal who is telling the truth. The difficulty of grasping the situation is made even more evident by the fact that Fonda's job as a journalist is to understand the events so that she can represent them to her listeners. However, the strikers' attempts to communicate their situation indicates how much communication assumes a shared background of experience, an assumption directly counter to the organisation of modern journalism. The shots which show Fonda and Montand as workers in the factory merely indicate the distance that separates them from the strikers.

Fonda represented as a worker.

However, the time in the factory forces Fonda and Montand to reflect on the reality of oppression in their own lives. She, as a journalist, has to face the fact that her report on the strike cannot include her own confusions but must assume a knowledge it doesn't have in order to qualify as journalism. He, as a film-maker, has to recognise that simply to abandon making films, as he had done after 1968, and to earn his living by using his technical skills to make advertising films is to avoid the reality of oppression and struggle at the level of his work. This evasion of the political is impossible and it is this lesson that Fonda drives home in the central scene in the film when, after their return to Paris, they have a row. Montand wants to divide his life into different compartments. Fonda, however, realises that such a division is impossible, that personal relations cannot be divorced from the other practices with which they are articulated. In short, that one can understand subjectivity only in terms of class.

But, and here we come to the paradox of the film, if the film analyses the struggles that dominate our life in terms of an economic base and its inadequate political representation, it has no analysis of that economic base nor of the dominant political representations. If we must understand subjectivity in terms of class, the content of the notion of class is reduced to the slogan **'it is right to rebel'**. That economic analysis is joined to a political one in which the only representative of struggle at the level of politics is a communist party which is seen as nothing more than a repressive fiction. If **Tout va bien** is a truly remarkable political film in that it introduces its audience to some of the ideological and social struggles that composed France four years after 1968 (and this marks its superiority to **British Sounds** or **Pravda** which rarely, if ever, manage to articulate the struggles in Britain or Czechoslovakia), there is no place in the film to include the fact that the contemporaneous signing of the Common Programme by the parties of the left was to provide a political focus for those ideological and political struggles over the next five years.

This weakness is exemplified in the third section, 'France Today', in which the lessons of the film are spelt out at a national level. Images and sounds of revolt from throughout France are followed by images and sounds of consumption as Fonda visits one of the huge hypermarkets situated on the outskirts of towns which had just begun to open in the early 1970s. If the use of the camera had prevented many of the traditional identifications we experience in the cinema, the organisation of the narrative still privileges one view. In the factory it is the strikers: their personal appearance, their relaxed manner of speaking and their obvious solidarity contrast with the repressed and repressive appearance of the manager and the shop

The manager of the factory being timed for a visit to the toilet by one of the strikers.

From **Tout va bien**

From **Tout va bien**

steward. It is Fonda who becomes the representative of the strikers in the rest of the film as in the row with Montand she demonstrates that she has learnt the lesson of their experience better than he. In the final scene as we see her walking through the hypermarket, her voice-over commentary, which represents the report that she is unable to write in the forms offered to her by journalism, can be read as nothing less than the summary of the film's conclusions. If the strength of the film is its insistence that we cannot separate our personal lives from the contemporary economic, political and social struggles, its weakness is its assertion of the dominance of a politics whose only content is finally a random violence. The political question that Fonda asks in the hypermarket is **'Where do we begin to struggle against the compartmentalisation of our lives?'** The answer is the morally powerful but politically vacuous, **'Everywhere at once'.** But insofar as the film insists that it is political, this vacuity must be given a content. The content of politics is provided by an image which acts, in the most traditional way, as the visible evidence of the truth of Fonda's voice-over. Into the hypermarket where a communist party member is selling copies of the party's programme erupt a group of leftists. After taunting the communists, they ransack the hypermarket. The image of revolt finally enters into the image of consumption.

This emphasis on violence which is the final political conclusion of **Tout va bien** runs through all the Dziga-Vertov films and is present before then in **La Chinoise** and **Weekend.** At the time of its appearance **La Chinoise** was virulently attacked by Maoists, whose principal objection was that the emphasis on terrorism at the end of the film was in total contradiction with the political analysis provided by Maoism. But Godard's analysis has, in the long run, proved more accurate than it seemed at the time. Terrorism was in contradiction with traditional Leninist emphases and with Mao Tse-tung's teaching. However, Western Maoism's rejection of all intermediate economic and political demands and the subsequent inevitability of betrayal by the delegate provided by the union or the communist party did often leave violence as the only political strategy. Much of the glorification of the violence in these films is objectionable. Nevertheless, ten years later, when a pessimistic view might discern terrorism as the only visible heritage of

'68, Godard's analysis seems much more acute than his supposedly more politically sophisticated detractors allowed at the time.

If Godard has never explicitly criticised this feature of his films, **Letter to Jane** does criticise the privileging of Fonda in **Tout va bien,** although it is unfortunate that this criticism is mainly aimed by the directors at Fonda rather than at themselves. The film is not explicitly about **Tout va bien** but about a photograph of Jane Fonda in North Vietnam which appeared in the pages of most of the Western press in August 1972. **Letter to Jane** analyses the photograph and the text that appeared with it in the French weekly *L'Express* in order to reflect both on the status of the image and on the problem, central to **Tout va bien,** of the relations of intellectuals to the revolution. The film takes the form of a montage of still photographs over which Godard and Gorin speak a commentary. Although the photograph is considered from a number of different perspectives (its composition, the text that accompanies it, its relation to film images and so on), its message is finally very simple. Whatever the good reasons that the Vietnamese have for ensuring that the photograph receives world-wide distribution, from Fonda's point of view the photograph simply crystallises a relation to the revolution that **Tout va bien** criticised. She is used as a star by the Vietnamese instead of examining in her own life as an actress the lessons of the Vietnamese revolution. The film explicitly criticises **Tout va bien** when it considers the expression on Fonda's face in terms of the history of the cinema. Godard and Gorin claim that this expression, developed in Hollywood concurrently with the technological development of the talkies and the political development of Roosevelt's New Deal policy, is one of compassionate understanding which lacks all specificity. They further state that Fonda's expression in the factory in **Tout va bien** was the same expression again and that therefore **Tout va bien** had failed.

Letter to Jane is both a very interesting and, often, a very objectionable film. Its greatest problem, which it attempts to avoid by mentioning, is that it is a

From **Letter to Jane**

Jane Fonda listens to the women workers in **Tout va bien**

Film stills used in **Letter to Jane**

News photograph used in **Letter to Jane**

★My discussion of **Letter to Jane** owes much to Anthony McCall's and Andrew Tyndale's remarkable film *Argument.*

criticism by two men of the way that a woman has chosen to use her image politically. This repressive tone is confirmed when in the section on the history of the cinema Jane's expression is represented as a simple imitation of her father. At the same time, however, its concern with the contemporary status and historic development of the image entails a re-engagement with the dominant forms of the image's dissemination but now widened to include photographs, and particularly their use in the news, as well as the more traditional cinematic image. The film also addresses a new audience which is constituted neither by the cinema nor by politics but rather by a shared history which includes both and, specifically, the film **Tout va bien.** This new definition of the audience might be considered as a narrowing or merely an indulgence but it is one that will allow Godard to examine most directly his own pre-occupations in which politics and the cinema both figure but which can be more precisely defined in terms of the examination of sound and image. At the same time the film often lags behind its own practice in that the sound-track still assumes a correct line, still assumes a political audience which the very strategy of the film casts in doubt. ★

Ici et ailleurs elaborates many of the more positive elements in **Letter to Jane** and constitutes a more thorough-going critique of the Dziga-Vertov group films. Using material shot for **Jusqu à la victoire,** it intercuts images of the Palestinian revolution with images of a contemporary French family watching television. Over these images Godard and Miéville discuss the intentions that Godard had in 1970 and the lessons that can be learned from these images and those intentions. Perhaps the film's most telling emphasis is the repeated cry, **'the sound is too loud'.** When, in 1970, Godard went to Palestine to find images of the revolution that had never been seen in France, the sound (the political analysis, the practice of the Dziga-Vertov group) was too loud, so loud that it was impossible to see these images in relation to the quotidian images of France, so loud that it was impossible to see one's own activity in the image, finally too loud even to see what was in the image itself. This oppressive and blinding dominance of the political is most movingly evoked in a sequence in which Palestinian guerrillas practise a military manoeuvre. In three months all the members of the group would be dead, killed in the September massacres, and for Godard and Miéville it is evident, in retrospect, that these images of them training are literally images of life and death. But at the time Godard had been unable to see this, blinded by a sound so loud that revolutionary correctness was the only message that the image could convey.

Indeed, it is a re-emphasis on the image which marks both **Ici et ailleurs** and the subsequent films, a concern to understand the workings of the image in our lives, the way in which the image enriches and impoverishes us. It is this emphasis rather than the sound of Maoism that determines the strategy of the later films. If Maoism finally produced a dominance of the political where the aim had been to subvert the political, Godard's programme is now to hold a variety of practices in balance, playing one against another through his own activity as an image-maker without awarding primacy to any one of them. Thus **Numéro deux's** indecision as to whether it is a sex movie or a political movie is an index of its commitment not to reduce the terms of the one to the other.

Stills from **Ici et ailleurs** used in **Photos et Cie**

It would be a mistake to say that politics has disappeared from Godard's work; it remains one of the elements. But Godard has drawn, in particularly stark form, some of the bitter consequences of the failure of the revolutionary left in Europe during the 1970s. For Godard questions of sexuality and technology are as immediate and as vital as any explicitly political questions. One might point to feminism and the increasing importance of the ecology movement as instances of the fact that questions of sexuality and technology must take political forms but Godard's answer might well be that one cannot find any form able to comprehend all these movements that will not finally reduce them.

Leninist politics forecloses all questions of ethics; Godard's recent films reintroduce them. Not in the form of a series of universal moral laws, Maoist or otherwise, nor still less in terms of some utilitarian calculus of pleasure and pain, but rather in a form, intellectually familiar from Nietzsche, but more readily available in a variety of popular radical traditions, of an emphasis on confronting one's own determinations in an encounter for which no else can prepare you. The films work towards a recognition of solitude: Godard's and our own. The economic determinants that circumscribe and lessen our lives now begin to appear as immutable; unchangeable by even the most radical politicisation. For Sandrine in **Numéro deux** it is unimportant whether Pierre is going to work or to join a picket line. In the film-making as in the films the primacy of practice in its heterogeneous forms is now reaffirmed. If Maoism promised to find some common determinant which could unify these practices, to provide a theory and a politics, it finally threatened to diminish them. For Godard it is true that we must start everywhere at once but there are now no necessarily common terms which will make our everywheres coincide in the possibility of political action.

Colin MacCabe:
The problems of the forms of politics and the problems of the forms of Hollywood cinema seem indistinguishable in your early work. **Made in USA** appears almost as a conscious last try to put the two together: Nick Ray and Sam Fuller plus politics. Did you feel that at the time?

Jean-Luc Godard:
There were too many things, things were too mixed up. I wanted to say too many things or to prove something. I don't know what it was . . . to feel and to prove together . . . I don't know.

I think that the political thinking that went with the Dziga-Vertov films is fairly evident but I'd like to know more about the specific reasons that you made **Tout va bien.**
It was more of a Gorin thing. I mean, I was not raised in politics. A lot of the friends I had or the people I know — their parents were militants, they heard the Internationale at the age of two. I was going to church. Later I discovered that it was the same thing and they only pretended that it was different. For me Mao was just someone who was contradictory — who said that you couldn't equate socialism with Russia. Even now the terrorists are still for me the inheritors. It's like families. It took me a long time to leave my family. Until I was twenty-two I tried to grab, to be secure, to take all of it. Then I was obliged to leave. I was thrown out. If nobody's throwing me out then I stay in the same place. I don't move of my own accord. I don't want to move. But

then I act in that same place in such a way that I'm obliged to move because the place or the people make me move because they don't want to see me not moving in that particular way. And a lot of young militants . . . Gorin, for example, it was funny because he has a lot of family problems, father problems, mother problems. And it was the same with politics — Marx or the father. I just heard of someone named Mao who seemed to me to be part of the New Wave. He said things differently and the few of his texts that I read, very few, made me work to think in a way that no other political texts ever did. And I was interested but not in the same sense that other people were . . .

So the decisions as to what kind of films to make — militant films or popular films like **Tout va bien** — you didn't participate in those decisions?

I disagreed with most of them because I said movies must be made in this way and they said 'Who cares about movies? We care about the people.'

But those were disagreements with other film-makers on the left. I'm asking about decisions within the Dziga-Vertov group, how you and Gorin planned your work.

Well, at that time he had a problem. I was more his father. This happens again and again. Anne-Marie (Miéville) is out of it, she can say: 'In *Pierrot le fou* this is not bad but this is very bad'. Other people, especially men, are too overwhelmed by the name. The public, the cultural public, don't make movies. They pretend. They pretend they know about movies, that they know who is good and who isn't. But in any relationship with me they have too much respect and too much admiration, which is ruinous. You can't have a normal relationship, you're constantly being put in an elevated position. Gorin broke with me over money but it was also because I was too heavy but he had brought that heaviness on himself. I was making movies with him but I was his father. And perhaps there's something in me that deserves that response. I don't like it.

There's a certain glorification of violence and terrorism which runs through your movies which I find very repellent. Like at the end of **Tout va bien** — Fonda asks 'What's politics?' and the image replies 'Ransacking a supermarket'.

That was French 'gauchisme' and anyway the end of 'gauchisme'. It's because movies should be done more naturally. Perhaps on TV, but then that 'naturalness' is so unnatural that I don't really know whether you could do it. With movies it's one and a half hours and ten years — it's too much.

76

Eisenstein's *Battleship Potemkin* was about 1905; it was made twenty years later — that's too much. And then it becomes a masterpiece and that limits things because once you've got one masterpiece then all the other films become 'not masterpieces'.

A lot of what you've just said seems to distance you from politics. And yet your films and your writings still insist on politics. In **Ici et ailleurs,** you try to understand the 'and' between the revolution in Palestine *and* the consumer society in France, between images of revolution *and* images of consumption. Or, in the 300th number of *Cahiers du Cinéma* that you've edited, the magazine ends with a directly political statement: **'On whom does repression depend — on us. On whom does liberation depend — on us.'**

Yes, yes but . . . politics has been so used, so misused and I feel that I have used it too much because I bought it under false pretences. Yes, Ici et ailleurs is finally devoted to evolving values for what's in between. I consider myself much more in terms of between than in terms of some fixed place. I think and I work better when I'm travelling — when you're supposed to be doing nothing. Sometimes I need two hours to get to the station. To go five minutes before kills me. That's not moving . . . you're in one place then you rush to another one and between them doesn't exist. For me it's the between that exists and the places are more immaterial. The camera is a between but because it's a solid object, people, movie people, don't think it's real communication. They think travel is just showing your ticket. They forget the between but the camera is a between, between what goes in and what comes out; the camera is communication in a solid state.

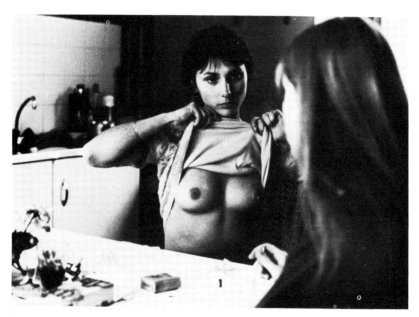

From **Sauve qui peut**

Laura Mulvey and Colin MacCabe

4: IMAGES OF WOMAN, IMAGES OF SEXUALITY.

'Do you know, madame, that despite your very light brown hair, you make me think of a beautiful redhead. *La Jolie Rousse* is a poem by Apollinaire. "Soleil voici le temps de la raison ardente . . .". Well, that burning-bright reason which the poet is looking for . . . when it does appear, it takes on the form of a beautiful redhead. That is what can be seen on a woman's face, the presence of awareness, something which gives her a different, an extra beauty. Feminine beauty becomes something all-powerful, and it's for that reason, I believe, that all the great ideas in French are in the feminine gender'.

From **Une Femme mariée**

Are there objects which are inevitably a source of suggestiveness as Baudelaire suggested about women?

Barthes

'Following this line of thought, one might reach the conclusion that women have escaped the sphere of production only to be absorbed the more entirely by the sphere of consumption, to be captivated by the immediacy of the commodity world no less than men are transfixed by the immediacy of profit . . .

The ultimate kitchen.

You are looking at what we call in Germany "Die Perfekt-Front". It means the overall effect of the specially chosen and matched, solid wood veneers that Poggenpohl use for every kitchen.

In fact, less than 50% of the wood that our suppliers feel comes up to *their* standards comes up to *our* standards.

It may sound wasteful, but the end result allows us to claim that we do make the ultimate kitchen.

We even continue the veneer onto shelf edging and on all visible structural surfaces to complete the effect.

But the beauty of Poggenpohl is much more than just skin deep.

Examine the superb design and meticulous engineering. The use that's made of every inch of storage space. The smoothness of the sliding cupboards and drawers. The hang of the doors.

And the durability and texture of the work surfaces.

Cherry is just one of Poggenpohl's finishes. There are 28 others. All to the same unmatchable standard.

Come and see the ultimate kitchen at your nearest Poggenpohl Studio. But first, post the coupon below to: Poggenpohl U.K. Ltd., (C1) Kings Avenue House, New Malden, Surrey.

Please send me:
☐ The lavishly illustrated, 140 page Poggenpohl Catalogue containing all 29 beautiful colours and finishes of over 900 different units - for which I enclose £1 towards post and packaging:
☐ Name and address of my nearest stockist who will supply my Catalogue free.

Name

Address

C1

poggenpohl

80

Elizabeth Arden introduces
the first personalized makeup:

"FLAWLESS FINISH"

Sponge-On Cream Makeup.

You command the coverage,
you control the finish,
because you damp-sponge
it on. From rich coverage
for all-out glamour, to
the lightness of the soft,
sheer nature girl look.
This is the fresh,
flawless finish that
lasts and lasts.
The new moisture-
enriched makeup
for today's
many faces.

Elizabeth Arden

. . . Women mirror the injustice masculine society has inflicted on them — they become increasingly like commodities'.

Adorno on Veblen

PIRELLI

M	T	W	T	F	S	S	M	T	W	T	F	S	S
January	1	2	3	4	5	6	7	8	9	10	11
12	13	14	15	16	17	18	19	20	21	22	23	24	25
26	27	28	29	30	31

In the twenty years that Godard has been making movies one of the remarkable features of his work is its closeness to the contemporary moment. Perhaps the most striking example of this is **La Chinoise,** apparently aberrant when it appeared, yet confirmed in its actuality less than a year later by the events of May 1968. But all his films are inextricably locked in with the moment of their making, existing on the sharp edge between observing the world taking and changing shape and, in giving it concrete form in representation, being part of the changing shapes.

During these twenty years, and particularly in the last ten, feminism has emerged as a crucial new cultural and political force. Feminists have considered images and representations to be a political issue. Godard has always been in the forefront of debates on politics and representation. And women have always been central to his films. Yet, on this point, Godard's practice seems to be out of sync with feminist arguments on the representation of women. Perhaps the necessary exclusiveness of the women's movement, the need for women to develop their own positions, diminishes the influence of feminism on an established film-maker such as Godard, open, otherwise, to the political developments and conflicts of his moment. It is not that Godard's movies have remained untouched by the growth of feminism — quite the contrary — but his use of images of women continues from his early through his late films to raise problems for those who have followed the logic of feminist arguments. Two examples, from very different periods, can indicate both the interest and the problems of Godard's representations of women.

The first example goes straight to the heart of the matter. In **A bout de souffle** Patricia goes to a press conference given by the novelist M. Parvulesco, who has just published an erotic novel. He is surrounded by journalists bombarding him with questions about love and the relations between the sexes and his responses can be taken as enigmatic or simply banal. When Patricia asks, **'Do you believe that women have a role to play in modern society?'**, we recognise that the question is as clichéd as the others but, at the same time, through our knowledge of the narrative, that it represents a real dilemma for Patricia herself. Should she try to pursue her career as a journalist or let herself be absorbed into Michel's world, a gangster movie made up of violence and his love for her, on the run from the police but promising dreams of freedom and fortune in Italy? Parvulesco's answer is short and to the point. He takes off his glasses, leans forward, giving Patricia a privileged

From **A bout de souffle**

84

From **A bout de souffle**

From **Le Gai Savoir**

look, and says: 'Yes, if she is charming, and is wearing a striped dress and dark glasses.' Patricia answers his look with a complicit smile. The deliberate misunderstanding becomes the deliberate suggestion: women's contribution to the modern world can be measured according to their sex appeal. This is a point that Godard returns to repeatedly in his films. He sees the forces that mould women into a stereotype and reduce them to impotence; more than any other single filmmaker Godard has shown up the exploitation of woman as an image in consumer society. For Godard this image is the very basis of consumer society, a relation he captures in his description of the contemporary world as *la civilisation du cul* (the civilisation of the ass). But his own relation to that image raises further problems. The scene from **A bout de souffle** demonstrates but is also complicit with an equation of woman and sexuality. In his later work Godard breaks down the equation to reveal its construction — that is, how the female form and its connotations are used in the circulation of images. But this investigation always risks producing another equation in which women represent *the problem of sexuality in capitalist society*. And this position can be traced back to Godard's romantic heritage in which woman is divided into an appearance that can be enjoyed and an essence that is only knowable at risk, deceptive and dangerous.

Ten years later Godard made **British Sounds.** Nothing could be further from **A bout de souffle,** a gangster genre movie, commented on, distanced, but still strongly within the magnetic radius of Hollywood, than this relentless political investigation of Britain in 1969. As Godard used and transformed the gangster movie in **A bout de souffle,** so he uses and transforms the documentary in **British Sounds** and as **A bout de souffle** shows Godard influenced by Hollywood and bringing Hollywood to Europe, so **British Sounds** is a product of the period of revolutionary commitment around 1968 and Godard's rigorous application of current ideas to the cinema. Both in their different ways show his involvement with his moment and the necessary unity, for him, of theory and practice. The film critic becomes director, the political militant makes movies. This combination of theoretical rigour and commitment to applying theory in his films makes Godard continually fascinating, as one watches dilemmas, contradictions being tackled in the course of his films. But it is not only a commitment to the inter-relation of theory to practice that links **A bout de souffle** and **British Sounds;** a concern with the contemporary situation of women is common to both. After a long opening travelling shot along a production line of cars over which a voice pronounces a classic Marxist analysis of capitalism, the sound-track prefaces the next section by announcing that **'the relation between man and man is dependent on the relation between man and woman'.** The sounds of this second sequence are already more complex. While a middle-class woman's voice talks of the subjective benefits and problems of women's liberation, a working-class man's voice juxtaposes the discourses of politics and sexuality, the distance between the two grotesquely exemplified in his demand for the **'Marxism-Leninist analysis of the natural position to fuck'.** The images which accompany these voices con-trast with the populous and noisy factory floor that we have just seen. The opening shot is of a silent interior of a suburban house in which a naked woman moves from room to room and goes up and down stairs. This static shot is followed by another, this time a close-up of the body framed from waist to thigh, and the sequence ends with a head-and-shoulders shot of the woman talking on the telephone, her conversation repeating with minor differences what the woman's voice-over is saying. The struggle between images and sounds which composes the film starts here. If the image of the factory has a sound to go with it — the classic Marxist analysis of capitalism — there is no sound for these images of silence, of women. For Godard, the voice of women's liberation and the voice of Marxism cannot be simply added one to the other, not least because we haven't begun to look at the silence of the house, at the unspoken body of woman. But Godard's presentation of woman

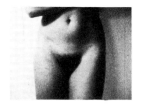

From **British Sounds**

86

simply identifies woman and sexuality, ignoring the evident fact that the contrast with labour in factory production would, in the home, be domestic labour, that of wife and mother as producer and reproducer of labour power, with the all-too-strident noises that accompany it. It is not that Godard's investigation lacks interest but it is finally a masculine investigation, ignoring the complex social determination of women's position in favour of an image of woman outside any social or economic context.

The limitations of Godard's position are evident in the images themselves. For many, the use of a naked female body immediately casts doubts on Godard's project. The very image for the most visible exploitation that women endure in a sexist society cannot be used with impunity, cannot be used without a certain complicity. Once again, the position is not straight-forward. It is possible to argue that Godard's use of the image of the body is resolutely unexploitative. The length of the shots and the fact that the image of the body is not presented as spectacle makes us uneasy in our position of the voyeur. If we look at this woman's body then we are aware of our own look, which is not hidden in the folds of the narrative and the movement of the camera. Similarly there is none of that titillation of vision on which exploitation depends. What we see is not the product of an unveiling; we gaze at a female body for several minutes. But although these arguments are valid they do not resolve the problem. The shot of the naked woman is a good example. On the one hand its length and form are an attempt to demystify the very source of our images of women and yet, at the same time, the potency of that image is such that it is doubtful that any simple demystification is possible. To use that image is immediately to run the risk of introducing the discourse in which the enigma of woman will offer the truth of the male situation; to reveal the truth of the image is to risk the inevitable demand for a true voice to complete it.

Godard slides continually between an investigation of the images of woman and an investigation which uses those images. It could be

From **British Sounds**

argued that since his collaboration with Miéville this sliding has to a certain extent diminished as the problems of male sexuality have been introduced directly into the content of the films. **Numéro deux** is the most important example of their collaboration, from this perspective, but before looking at **Numéro deux** Godard's earlier films should be considered.

It is illuminating to examine the effect that sexing of point of view has on the narrative of particular films. There is an important difference between films organised around a male central protagonist and those around a female one, a difference between the worlds they depict. Although this rule holds greater sway in Hollywood genre movies, its effect, infinitely more nuanced and sometimes consciously defied, ★ can also be seen in Godard's films. For instance, in **Pierrot le fou,** in which Ferdinand acts as central consciousness, the narrative referent is fiction and fantasy. The action does not develop in terms of logical relations of time, space and verisimilitude but in great sweeps (**'We crossed France'**), picaresque adventure (**'Look, Pierrot, a Ford Galaxy . . . Go on, show me you're a man'**), generic violence (**'detective stories'**) and utopian escape (**'the island of Mystery'**). On the other hand the narrative of **Une Femme mariée**, in which Charlotte acts as central consciousness, is acted out on a considerably smaller scale. Charlotte's story is literally a slice of life, with a beginning, middle and end, that is highly organised on the level of narrative form and symmetry, but not on the level of narrative action. The end provides no solution, no rounding off of the drama. And, unusually for Godard, there is no violence. The dramatic space of **Une Femme mariée** is social and analytic, emerging out of Rouch and Rossellini rather than Sam Fuller and *film noir*. Sometimes, as in **Masculin/Féminin,** for instance, the intimacy of the human relations observed is abruptly broken by bizarre outbreaks of violence. But this interweaving never merges two different worlds. Godard's use of space functions both figuratively and fictionally to limit the world of women's daydreams; it is only when pro-

★ Thus, for example, Anna Karina plays the Humphrey Bogart character in **Made in USA.**

From **Pierrot le fou**

From **Une Femme mariée**

From **Pierrot le fou**

jected in a man's fantasy that her body takes on an image of power. The spatial limitations introduced by the woman's point of view have no necessary link with 'realism', but Godard always uses this reduced space to analyse woman in relation to her social formation. Godard makes an important attempt to depict woman from 'inside', but this positioning always implies an 'outside', an alternative, masculine point of view from which woman's threatening qualities predominate. Her image does not relate to women but is a phantasm of the male unconscious, familiar as the Romantic image of *La Belle Dame sans merci* or as the heroine of the *film noir*. In **Pierrot le fou,** Marianne is the origin of violence. It is here that Godard views woman from outside in a fantasy based on fear and desire. She is mysterious, ultimately elusive, fascinating and destructive. This 'otherness' depends on our following the film's narrative from the hero's point of view.

From **Pierrot le fou**

89

Marianne is as mysterious to the spectator as to Ferdinand. She closely resembles the 'heroines' of Hollywood *film noir:* the hero leaves his home and family to follow her into a world of violence and *amour fou.* The film constantly refers to the *film noir* tradition: Marianne's frantic search for money seems to throw back to *Double Indemnity* (Wilder), her treachery to *The Lady From Shanghai* (Welles), her powers of destruction and self-destruction to *Out of the Past* (Tourneur). ★

Une Femme mariée presents a marked contrast to **Pierrot.** The spectator watches the development of the film alongside Charlotte; we *know* with her not with her husband or lover. But, at the same time, the image of Charlotte is distanced, re-presented as the problem of woman's image in consumer society. On the one hand Godard takes a situation recognisable through our own direct experience of life, dilemmas *within* society, similar to and familiar from the real world, and, on the other, he examines them in the image in order to demonstrate how far that direct experience is already an experience of images. The film's foregrounding of its own process of production and its break with the conventions of verisimilitude are not at the service of a formalist aesthetic. Rather, they produce an experience of the image which allows Godard to confront the way that consumer society moulds woman's image so that it conforms to a given concept of female sexual appeal.

The female body has become industrialised; a woman must buy the means to paint on (make-up) and sculpt (underwear/clothes) a look of femininity, a look which is the guarantee of *visibility* in sexist society for each individual woman. Advertisements sell the means of production of the look, sealing it in a given image of feminine desirability, attainable by means of lip-sticks, bras, scents and so on — magic formulae depending on novelty for appeal just as the market depends on turnover for profit. Magazines provide the know-how, techniques and expertise, sealing the association of *woman* and *sexuality* in the minds of

★ Sylvia Harvey (1978) has noted the crucial absence of the family in the *film noir*, and the association of woman with sexual excess and destruction.

un autre ?.. jamais... j'aime trop

Magazine images used in
Une Femme mariée

Film still used in **Une Femme mariée**

women themselves. It is almost as though woman herself were a factory, feeding in the means of production, painting on the mask and emerging transformed with value added in the process, a commodity ready for consumption. **Une Femme mariée** contains a great many references in dialogue to male concepts of female beauty and their mediation through the image:

Robert: **'You ought to do like they do in Italian films . . . Have you seen any? The women don't shave under their arms.'**

Charlotte: **'I prefer American films. Hollywood ones . . . they're prettier.'**

Robert: **'Yes, but less arousing.'**

There is also a recurrent emphasis throughout the films on images of the female breasts, from advertisements of brassieres to **'the ideal breasts of Venus de Milo',** and both Charlotte and Mme Céline try to measure themselves to see how they compare with this ideal figure.

From **Une Femme mariée**

Charlotte is nothing more than a perfect image. But this perfect image, this mask of visibility (which composed of make-up, clothes and so on, has an indexical relationship to the woman's body) is furthermore a symbolic sign. It represents the concept of woman in a given social formation — that is, the equation woman = sexuality. This feminine mask is the passport to visibility in a male-dominated world. ★ But Charlotte's look as object is fractured for the spectator insofar as he or she must assume her look as subject, her point of view, from which the image disintegrates and which cannot accommodate the world of her work (shot in negative). Her mask of visibility conceals behind it the diverse and complex nature of woman's place in the social and economic order, where sexual difference is a matter of division of labour, a difference and a division which has no image, no form. The invisible women in factories, homes, schools, hospitals, are formless and unrepresentable.

★ It is important to remember that the concept of femininity reproduced in the look is not the simple product of the advertising agencies but is caught in a complex relationship with the whole tradition of representation of women. It is male obsessions and desires which achieve tangible form in novels, poems, paintings, movies, pin-ups, cartoons, providing the 'look' with a model.

From the photo-call sequence which Charlotte attends in **Une Femme mariée**

As observer of woman as image and analyser of the moulding, masking process evolved by consumer capitalism, Godard is acute and rigorous. His consciousness of image as cultural product, consciousness of himself as part of and torn by cultural traditions, gives him an awareness of the levels of meaning that the image of woman has acquired in history like the grime on an ancient monument. He advances the argument another important step further. In **Une Femme mariée,** Godard is interested in the relationship between advertising and the body, the commodities produced for women and the image which sells the commodities. He then indicates how that image functions in relation to the home and to the place of the woman in the home as *the* consumer in advanced capitalist society. Charlotte and Pierre present their apartment to their dinner guest in the language of the advertising brochure. The image on the screen, showing Pierre sitting down on the sofa next to Charlotte, establishes Godard's perception of the married couple as the basic unit of consumer capitalism, and the home they construct about them as its crucial market outlet. The married woman's function is to provide a rationale for this economic process, and simultaneously to be, herself, *prima inter pares* of her husband's possessions. Her body's mass-produced perfection expresses his position in the world outside, the world of production and achievement.

From **Une Femme mariée**

Traditionally, it has been within the bourgeoisie that a woman's physical appearance, elegance and fashionability have complemented her husband's economic position. Illustrating the shifts inherent in the changing nature of 'subsistence' under capitalism, **Deux ou trois choses** concentrates not on the bourgeoisie as in **Une Femme mariée,** but on the effects of consumer capitalism on the Parisian working class. The family lives in a new housing estate, a concrete jungle on the outskirts of the city, a new world similar to that of **Une Femme mariée;** but the different social context is indicated by the fact that the husband is a car mechanic rather than a pilot. In **Deux ou trois choses** the landscape functions as *mise-en-scène*, echoing the changing world around Juliette. In **Une Femme mariée** the language and landscape of advertising seemed to shape people and their lives like a sculpting force. In **Deux ou trois choses** the landscape has become gigantic, disproportionate to the people who scuttle like ants among motorways and housing complexes. The screen of **Deux ou trois choses** is filled with earthmovers and bulldozers which are changing the city's spatial relations. The anthropomorphic proportions of Paris are disappearing. As Godard's voice announces on the sound-track:

'one thing is obvious: that the structuring of the Paris region will enable the government to carry out its class policy with even greater ease and that the monopolies will be able to direct and organise the economy without really taking into account the aspirations to a better life of those eight million inhabitants'.

In other words no normal life
From **Deux ou trois choses**

The film is set at the moment when luxury goods came within the economic sphere of the working class, during the boom in consumer durables (before rampant inflation, before depression). Once again Godard sees advertising as playing a crucial role in forming people's desires, creating a new market for expanding production. Once again, the family and the home are the point of consumption and it is the wife's job to 'manage' the process. In **Deux ou trois choses,** loosely based on a news item that attracted Godard's attention, the wife, Juliette, takes to casual prostitution to earn the extra money needed to keep up with this new 'image' of a correct standard of living. **Deux ou trois choses** marks a move away from the exotic perception of a woman's selling of her sexuality present in **Vivre sa vie** or **Une Femme est une femme,** where the heroine is a stripper. However, the centrality of sexuality to any

93

image of woman is, if anything, more marked in **Deux ou trois choses.** Godard's perception of women in the economy is simultaneously illuminating and obscurantist. His analysis of the place of the image in relation to consumption, to our patterns of living, is acute and succeeds in linking the oppression of capitalism and the alienation of sexuality. There is, however, a crucial flaw in the analysis because, although it shows up the close relations between sexuality and an economic system, it finally reproduces the equation between woman and sexuality which, at another level, it displaces. If one series of Godard's films assumes a woman's point of view, it is a point of view that is determined by her sexuality. In the tradition of the apocryphal Jesuit dictionary containing the entry '*Woman:* see *Sin*', Godard's films conflate woman and sexuality. With the very important exception of **Tout va bien** Godard never shows women placed in an economic or social role that is not an aspect of their sexual function or its social rationalisation, marriage. It is as though woman can only be of interest only through her sexuality. At the point where the most rigorous challenge is necessary, Godard's own cultural traditions, the legacy of romanticism, his place in a system of desire, overdetermine his analysis of woman. Going back to **Pierrot,** escape from the confines of the home, the advertising language of his elegant wife and friends, lies for Ferdinand in the world of fantasy: 19th-century romanticism or 20th-century cinema or strip cartoons. And in this cultural tradition woman, once again, becomes the sign for the sexual desires and fears of men. The phantasm appears again, an image of mystery, essential otherness and, very often, violence and deceit. From **Pierrot** until 1968 this crisis became more and more acute. Godard's attempt to articulate the cultural traditions of classical art and the popular cinema was disintegrating under the more immediate pressures of the war in Vietnam. It was no longer possible to separate the romantic violence of Hollywood from the violence of imperialism, and the high cultural traditions from Velazquez to Picasso lead to a

From **Pierrot le fou**

beautiful but arid dead-end on a Mediterranean island, cut off from history. In the more political films that followed, the privileging of sound over image went together with, one could almost say determined, a decreased interest in images of woman.

Indeed, Godard did not return specifically to the question of women until 1975, when he made **Numéro deux** in collaboration with Anne-Marie Miéville. It is his most thorough and self-conscious attempt to depict the problem of sexuality under capitalism, but at the same time leaves the spectator with a sense of hesitancy and pessimism. The changes brought about in the working-class family by the post-war development of capitalism seem to have stabilised. Goods which, in **Deux ou trois choses,** might have stood for the *embourgeoisement* of the consumer boom, such as a television or a washing-machine, are now part of the basic subsistence of working-class life. Pierre's earphones for listening to music appear to be his status symbol. The concrete blocks of flats mush-rooming everywhere in the earlier films have grown roots and lost any promise of a new way of life. In fact, the new way of life is one of claustrophobic imprison-ment. Godard's old sensitivity to the limits of women's mobility in the world now focuses on the rigid division between inside and outside. The housewife is tied more tightly to the home and the camera echoes her im-prisonment, never moving outside the confines of the flat, except to show her once, returning from a doomed search for work, refusing to give her attention to the demands of the outside world, refusing to listen to a woman campaigner for Chile. The camera registers this scene from the balcony above, maintaining its own sense of imprisonment. This same camera position is used for the other exterior scene in the film. Emphasis-ing the interior/exterior division as one of sexual difference, the screen juxtaposes Pierre, in successive shots, leaving for and returning from work super-imposed over an image of Sandrine lying asleep in bed. The bed evokes a space more intimate yet more con-fined, the cosiness of the home inside the prison block,

From **Numéro deux**

but at the same time takes us back to essential associations between woman and sexuality.

Numéro deux opens with a long introductory sequence. First Godard himself presents the film, its apparatus (film and video combined) and its mode of capitalisation by his old friend and producer Georges Beauregard. Then the themes of the film are presented in a pre-diegetic ★ sequence. Using two video monitors with voice-over commentary and written titles, Godard brings together an assortment of ideas and images that are suggestive rather than coherently argued. Cinema, sex, politics are the recurring images that start to work together almost subliminally for the spectator but actually define quite explicitly the film's area of interest. One monitor shows documentary footage of a May Day parade, the other shows scenes from kung-fu movies, porno movies and trailers finally posing the issue (voice off): **'No, it's not about politics, it's about sex.' 'No, it's not about sex, it's about politics.'**

★ *diegesis:* the fictional world of the narrative

The diegetic section of the film keeps the video format, sometimes juxtaposing two monitor screens within the single cinematic space. The film uses rolling superimposition, direct superimposition and vision-mixing in which one image appears as an insert in another. This allows the action of the film to exist on different spatial levels simultaneously, developing a kind of montage within the single image itself, providing the spectator with the kind of pleasure in juxtaposition that can be obtained from the best use of deep-focus cinema.

Numéro deux is about the family unit, with the couple in the centre, children (a boy and a girl) coming after them and a grandmother and grandfather before them. Here we see the basic unit for production and reproduction of labour power, with the woman, in the home, the 'factory' that carries out the process. However, the film is not primarily concerned with the question of domestic labour under capitalism, but rather with the effects of capitalism on sexual relations and the oppression of the working class on this personal,

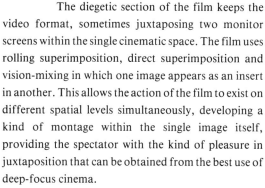

Images from **Numéro deux**

96

emotional level. Work is one factor that disrupts Pierre and Sandrine's enjoyment of sex. Pierre comes home reduced to virtual impotence by the hierarchical chain of command at the factory, and is unable to satisfy Sandrine (she says **'If I was rich I'd pay for it'**) or do more than feel a mixture of sympathy and resentment at her complaints. But there is also a theme which has been important in Godard's earlier works involving relations between the sexes: that of female deception and the violence provoked as a result. Pierre rapes Sandrine anally in revenge for her sleeping with another man. The scene is probably the most important in the film, repeated often with varied presentations, unequivocally shown as a scene of male violence and assault on a woman and a scene witnessed by their little daughter Vanessa.

Pierre: **'One day something terrible happened. Sandrine had fucked another guy. She wouldn't tell me who. I wanted to rape her. She let me and finally I buggered her. Then she started screaming. Afterwards we realised that Vanessa had seen it all. I suppose that's what family life is all about'.**

The little girl's witnessing of this act of sexual violence reproduces a cliché, shocking in its visual realisation, of Freud's concept of the primal scene. But the presence of the little girl acts almost as a distraction from the underlying force and importance of the rape. It is here that Godard shows the hatred and disgust, the virulent rejection of sexual difference, that brings the romantic concept of woman to life. It is only a moment of violence that gives Pierre sexual potency. Later on he says **'Sometimes she is the man and I am the woman. But seeing that I'm a guy, sometimes with her it's . . . it's as though I was fucking another guy. It must be because I like her putting her finger up my arse. I often ask her to do it.'**

It is these moments that mark a crucial shift in the terms of Godard's presentation of sexuality. For the first time the chickens came home to roost. The problem of sexuality is not *wholly* signified by a woman; the problems of male sexuality, and the

Images from **Numéro deux**

attendant undercurrents of misogyny and violence, come out into the open. Godard and Miéville now explicitly investigate the nature of the male sexuality that turns woman into an image of its desire and, crucially, the repression of homosexuality as one of the founding moments of that sexuality. The violence against women, the emphasis on anal sex, turns around this ambiguous relation to other men. It is another man's penis in Sandrine's body that turns it into an object of desire but also into an object that must be punished for arousing that desire. It could be objected that Godard's treatment of this problem presents this repression and the subsequent violence as inevitable. In one of the key scenes of the film the mother and daughter dance while the son is eating. When the mother attempts to persuade the boy to join them, she is angrily repulsed in a gesture of sexual shame and disgust. This image of male self-exclusion from a female world in which the body is more easily accepted is one that recurs in the script of **The Story** and in **Sauve qui peut.**

There is a sense in which **Numéro deux,** at its most pessimistic, shows people trapped within a given sexual identity which they neither understand nor have any hope of transcending, and breeding a new generation into the same pattern. And the given sexual identity is sealed, not by personal desire, but by the needs of the social formation that defines their lives. It is not a question of conditioning: both Pierre and Sandrine are bitterly aware of their own shortcomings and seem to intuit the source as coming from outside themselves. But as an isolated unit imprisoned in a concrete block they can do no more than act out their anger against one another. Pierre attacks Sandrine. Sandrine rejects Pierre. The film shows the interconnected frustrations of sex and violence as permeating every aspect of 'ordinary' life. This is, perhaps, one of its more radical points: a relentless insistence on *showing,* on the cinema screen, the place of sex in the home: in front of the children, explained to the children, mystified to the children, part of everyday

Images from **Numéro deux**

98

language, the nudity of the young, the nudity of the old and so on.

In **Une Femme mariée** and **Deux ou trois choses,** Godard showed woman within a social formation, her sexuality functioning as part of an economic chain. In the second part of **Numéro deux,** Sandrine takes on a rather more symbolic function. Whereas the first part of the film is dominated by the image of the anal rape, the second part is dominated by Sandrine's constipation:

'When you can't get on with a man you can always leave him. But what do you do when it's a state? When a whole social system rapes you?'

Her blocked body comes to stand for the blockage in the social system as a whole; she consumes but she cannot produce. She eats but she is unable to shit. Sandrine is simultaneously at the bottom of the line, a woman defined by passivity, and elevated, as the image of woman has so often been elevated before, to an abstraction or an emblem. Godard and Miéville are centring the issue on Sandrine, positing that sexuality is not fantasy and escape from the 'inside' into day-dreams and fiction, but is rooted deeply into the home. Sandrine has her own desires beyond what she may represent for men but there is a sense in which she seems to become an empty sign for male desires. The film cannot be criticised for choosing to deal with one aspect of life rather than another, but the tendency to define woman in terms of sexuality, however much that definition is socially mediated, is familiar from Godard's earlier films, remembering once again the important exception of **Tout va bien.** Working-class women have always worked before and after child-rearing — and often during it — and play a vital part in the labour force. The fact that their image is fixed in the home, the reluctance of the labour movement itself to recognise women at work in production and services, is like yet another level of masking: women visible in relation to man, invisible in the factories, hospitals, offices and so on. Woman's vulnerable place in pro-duction is linked to her place in the home, producing and reproducing labour power, but both are two sides of the same coin. It is evocative to remember the first film ever shot — the Lumière brothers' record of workers leaving their factory. Most of the people going out of the factory gates on that day in 1895 were women.

There is another juxtaposition in **Numéro deux** that Godard and Miéville suggest and yet seem to skirt around. The two old people, grandmother and grandfather, have their own moments to speak. Both are shown naked, the woman washing accompanied by her voice off, the man sitting at a table with a drink and speaking straight to camera. The woman's speech is about woman, divided into two parts, seeming to represent the two sides of the paradox. The first part is about oppression and woman as victim of male violence, the need for her, herself, to make things change. The second part is about violence done to the natural world in the name of female narcissism, a litany of death and destruction for the adornment of her body. The man's speech is about his experience in the world, journeys to distant lands, adventure, politics and class consciousness. Here again one sees the spatial difference between male and female expectations of life, one tied to the body and the other free to roam and take action. This paradox takes us back to the original point of departure, the difference between the spatial representation of social relations in **Une Femme mariée** and fantasy in **Pierrot le fou.** But both depictions exist themselves within the institution of cinema and within (though in opposition to) a definite cultural tradition. Gradually a question seems to emerge, the question that Godard has always offered, the hardest to face, apparently impossible to answer: how can we effect a conscious and political interaction between the cultural forms of representation on the one hand and economic and social relations on the other? How does one affect the other? Should one show what is, what should be or the dreams that evade the other two? All these questions pose the issue of the relations between a real (the mask produced for women by society) and a

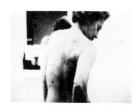

Images from **Numéro deux**

100

fantasy (the phantasm projected by men) and how those relations are caught in the image. This conjuncture has always fascinated Godard and has acted as a key point for his inquiries.

In **Numéro deux,** despite the radical presentation of sex and the family, Sandrine's body is shown without questioning traditional uses of female beauty and sexual allure in the dominant forms of image production. Yet the film rigorously undercuts its own imagery by its refusal of the use of an image which we can simply gaze at. Female nakedness carries associations of the exploitation of women that almost no degree of formal subversion can displace. How far can the fragmentation of the image in **Numéro deux,** reminiscent in some ways of the fragmentation of Charlotte's body in **Une Femme mariée,** undercut the iconography of woman contained within the separate images?

The contradictions apparent within Godard's depiction of women, the contradiction between his use of the female form to signify sexuality and his rigorous questioning of the film form itself constitute a statement of the confusions and difficulties surrounding images of woman. This lack of coherence is a productive springboard both as a starting point for understanding how and why woman's image accumulates its particular meanings and also as a basis for further development, the construction of a cinema which challenges those meanings and assumptions.

Images from **Numéro deux**

Colin MacCabe:

Your early films seem to use two different images of women. On the one hand there's woman as enigma and mystery, Marianne in **Pierrot le fou.** On the other there's woman as consumer, Charlotte in **Une Femme mariée.** Does that distinction seem valid?

Jean-Luc Godard:

Probably . . . it depends . . . But I think that my originality is that I don't make any distinction between men and women. It's just like two kinds of animals. I put my direction and my lines in a man's body and a man's mouth or in a woman's body and a woman's mouth without worrying that because she's a woman she can, or because he's a man he can't, say it. Sometimes I put my philosophy in three different characters whereas most directors have their own character. If they're on the left then one character represents their point of view and the other one plays ping pong. That was the difficulty that people had in understanding *Le Petit Soldat :* that my own opinion was not expressed by any one of the characters. People expect you to be for this character's view or that character's view. I say I'm for the picture. Renoir did the same in some pictures, *La Grande Illusion,* for example, and people didn't understand what was going on. I say what I've got to say in any kind of mouth that I like. If it's woman, it's a woman. I don't think about whether it should be a man or a woman.

The image of prostitution is very important in your early films. Around the time of **Deux ou trois choses** it becomes the all-important metaphor for contemporary society.

It was. Because sometimes it's easier to have a love relationship for money. It's hundredth of a second. In marriage it's a whole lifetime and maybe you don't really have much more. So there's something that's wrong but it's the truth of what's wrong, it's real. And then there's another problem that I can't really express: you have to talk. Particularly if you live in a city or are enslaved by the fact that more and more people are dominated by cities. And that means that you can't just sit and look and say something. Most of the things that I want to say, nobody is interested in hearing. Sometimes you can talk with money-makers or technicians but not for very long because it becomes too specialised. You just talk of money-making or technical questions.

Were you conscious in films like **Une Femme mariée** of telling the woman's story from her point of view?

No. But it's a fact that my women characters are stronger than the men.

102

The title of **Numéro deux** is a pun that indicates the two main themes of the title: women and shit. But isn't the concern with anality simply transposed on to the concern with women? The woman just becomes a metaphor instead of being the real subject of the film.

Yes, sure, sure. You know that picture by Cassavetes, *A Woman under the Influence* **? Well, all my film's are made under the influence. Perhaps it's the weather, perhaps it's . . .** *Numéro deux* **was made under the influence of Miéville. She wasn't there and she was angry because I'd taken a lot from her and I said to her that I'd always done that. If I make a picture of the sun I'd take from the sun. I can't produce things from myself. I don't know how other film-makers do it. I'm always taking, I never invent.**

Is your criticism of images of women in consumer society contaminated by the fact that you reproduce certain images?

Yes, sure. I was both criticising it but using it in the same way. I understand. But I think women should do more pictures. Men control too much. I try to make pictures like other people cook. To make enough time that one doesn't have to go to a snack bar or have to make hamburgers and salad. You have to have time to enjoy it. I explain to people that I don't enjoy cooking because you only have one life and you only have time to enjoy one thing. That's why I say to Anne-Marie, 'Finding the money to make a picture is the same as making a salad for you'. But you can't have both together. We're too small. We're just human bodies and human bodies are at maximum half, they're never entire. I'm always amazed when people say — it comes from Descartes, but you say it in your questions — 'I think that'. I always wonder how someone can say 'I' like that. I think I'm the only person, apart from perhaps Mao or other people that I haven't heard about, who thinks of himself as half, as not complete. Movies and communication help me to think that way and working together with someone else.

In your more recent projects there's more and more of an emphasis on children.

Of course. Because now I'm probably too old to have children. I'm looking at a real creation, a living creation . . . pictures, or books, or music are creations . . . from nothing. But they have a relationship. In the old days I very often spoke of my movies as babies. And for me to try to run a small production house is like Anne-Marie with the children. You see things beginning, you're obliged to be this and not that and learning and beginning to talk and to memorise. So I was interested by children and I was interested to understand what's wrong with the relation betwen work and love by looking at what children want. I know now that if I make a picture it's just to speak about what I'm

doing, about myself, but it's also giving something to other people so that they can take a part of me. But the normal production process makes sure that there's no more love in the work. It is supposed to be done with love. Work is a result of love and love is the result of work. And in the movies you can't have both. That's why it's always a love story. Because there's no more love. But people still love to go. But children . . . what do they want?

Mick Eaton and Colin MacCabe

At a time when the social debate is getting angrier and angrier — yet more coherent and specific, he looks very like a man huddling in the shelter of his gadgets — and only through gadgets, and machine-like presentation to admit that human warmth exists.

From a review of **Numéro deux** in the *Observer*, 30 January 1977

The lords of imperialism have transformed technology and sexuality into instruments of repression.

From **Le Gai Savoir**

Audience →

Fiction

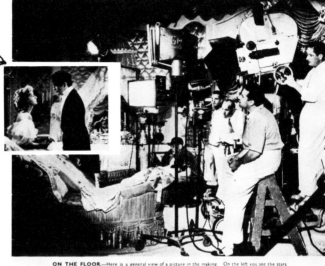

ON THE FLOOR.—Here is a general view of a picture in the making. On the left you see the stars GRETA GARBO and ROBERT TAYLOR. The director, GEORGE CUKOR, is seated by the camera in the right foreground. WILLIAM DANIELS, cameraman of most of the Garbo pictures, is behind the camera. Leaning on a stool in the background is the assistant director. The scene is the boudoir in "Camille."

Behind the Scenes . . . .

the director, discussing lighting, calling out instructions to the electricians up on high on the catwalks overhead, tending the big lamps that shine down on the scene. The man peering through the camera is more likely to be the cameraman's first assistant. The young man giving orders is the assistant director, responsible for seeing that everybody is on hand when wanted, for carrying out whatever the director wants, yelling or blowing his whistle when silence is needed for a rehearsal or a "take." Sitting with his headphones at a

switchboard nearby is the recording expert, in direct communication with the sound department to which the sound is carried by the microphone—see it there, the little black thing like a honey-comb hanging at the end of a boom, which is operated crane-fashion so that the "mike" can move easily and freely to whatever position is desired, even while the scene is being taken.

The stand-ins walk through the movements of the scene, the cameraman and director approve the lighting scheme, the stars take their places. The assistant director calls for silence. The red light outside the door is on now. Nothing

55

106

Exercise for the reader:

Try to put yourself
in the picture

From **Numéro deux**

Art is not the reflection of reality, it is the reality of that reflection.

From **La Chinoise**

To say that we live in a world of images is a commonplace of our age. But perhaps only Godard has taken this commonplace at its word and deduced that to displace the image is literally to destroy a world. Professional film-makers, reporters and the institutions which employ them seem concerned only to produce, relentlessly, even fearfully, more sounds and images for our consumption. Godard's work, particularly since 1968, has been concerned more with an interrogation of the sounds and images which prescribe our cultural horizons than with adding to their ceaseless production.

The advertisements for cameras shown here reflect the notion that the production of the photographic image is a unique combination of Art and Science, of aesthetics and technology — the intuitive eye of the artist and the mechanical laws of the instrument. The traces of this split are manifested throughout the range of institutions engaged in photographic, cinematic and televisual practice: the film artist as opposed to the film technician; the 'auteur' and the camera operator, the 'social message' of art and the neutrality of the technology required to produce that message.

At its worst this widely-held formulation carries with it the implication that the camera is merely an instrument to be used by the film-maker as a neutral tool for recording either the world as it exists 'out there' (in documentary films) or the expression of the film-maker's own peculiar and subjective view of the world (in fiction films or 'art cinema'). The specifications of photographic technology and the social and economic formations in which they are produced can have no determining influences on the 'messages' of the film or the ways in which they are received. As the advertising agency hired by the camera manufacturer tells us, 'Leave the technology to us — you invent the images'. But images of what? For whom?

Given this cultural context Godard's preoccupation in his life with cinematic and televisual technology, as well as his experiments with different,

'Leave the technology to us, you invent the images'

A chance to break into the system

The Art Machine

ads from **Photos et Cie**

more collaborative methods of making films, is dismissed by professional critics as an obsession with gadgetry. The questions his films raise about what it means to be a film-maker, and what it means to be a film-viewer, are condemned as idle self-indulgence. Moreover, this indulgence is seen as personally constipating, stopping Godard from involving himself in 'the real issues', from contributing to 'the social debate'.

We are asked to think that the development of cinematic technology has evidenced, especially in the last twenty years, a progression towards an increasingly unmediated relationship with reality — that the development of light, portable sync-sound cameras with the ability to film for longer periods of time and the increasing sophistication of video equipment has allowed the events of the world to be captured easily, directly and unproblematically. We are assured that the spectacular use of the latest technology can bring these events — the Olympics, the Iranian revolution, whatever — into our own living rooms, increasing our understanding of the world and bringing us closer together as citizens of the global village that the world has become. The picture editors of national newspapers and the makers of television documentary films tells us that a photograph can in itself sum up a decade, a war, a person, that a documentary film can show us what is happening in other parts of the world or in our own backyard.

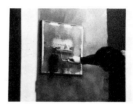

From **Tout va bien**

These are all ideological constructions that Godard has resolutely worked against in his film practice — **'cinema is not the reflection of reality, but the reality of that reflection'.** Cinema constructs meaning, it does not embody it, and the material apparatus of the cinema is integral to that construction. It is for that reason, not for some idiosyncratic indulgence, that cinematic technology is so often part of the pro-filmic event, the subject matter, in Godard's films, and that the cinematic institution's categories of 'documentary' and 'fiction' are so continuously thrown into crisis in the manipulation of that technology.

110

CE N'EST PAS UNE IMAGE JUSTE, C'EST JUSTE UNE IMAGE

Godard's famous maxim, **'Ce n'est pas une image juste, c'est juste une image'** (**'This is not a just image, it's just an image'**) insists on the fact that no image has a life of its own outside the institutions which exist to fix its meanings. Film does not exist as a neutral medium to convey messages which are independent, rather it finds its meanings in a series of social relations which place producer and consumer so that only certain meanings are possible. **'In every image we must know who speaks'** — thus Godard, and this imperative demands that we uncover the terms of address in the cinema, the terms in which we are constructed as spectators. Godard's films pose, as the French philosopher Gilles Deleuze has said, *'questions which silence answers'*, questions whose importance lies in the very fact that they disrupt and displace our routine ways of talking about the cinema. Questions which reveal that both the cinematic technology and the discourses which surround it and support it are fundamentally and profoundly ideological.

From the beginning of his career Godard has been concerned with — many of the technicians on his films might say obsessed with — cinematic techniques and technologies normally associated with direct cinema. Although he did not use 16mm cameras until 1965 — and then only for his short sketch for *Paris vu par* — the hand-held Cameflex, the sequence-length shot and, particularly, use of direct sound all feature prominently in his early films. Stories abound of his insistence, against conventional cinematic practice of the time, on naturalistic shooting. For example, Godard wanted to film **A bout de souffle** in natural light conditions. His cameraman, Raoul Coutard, who had been a still photographer, recommended using Ilford HPS stock for shooting in daylight with no extra artificial lighting. However, this was a stock for still cameras, not for the movies. So for the film they stuck together the 17½-metre lengths of the stock to make reels of the required length for motion-picture shooting and then shot with the relatively lightweight Cameflex as its sprocket holes corresponded most closely to those of a 35mm still camera. To process this they had to borrow a machine as no commercial laboratory could afford to develop at the speed they wanted, which was much faster than that normally required.

For **Une Femme est une femme** several sequences were shot in a studio — originally because this allowed easier camera manipulation during the lengthy and complicated sequence shots. However, when it came to the shooting Godard would not allow any of the walls to be moved and demanded that a ceiling be built for the set, allowing a more naturalistic claustrophobic space but removing all the advantages of shooting in a studio in the first place — especially as this was a colour film and colour stock is slow, a problem usually solved by overhead studio lighting. Although some use was made of direct sound for this film it was not until **Vivre sa vie** that a film was shot completely using sync-sound with only some of the music track of the film being post-synchronised. In several of the scenes only one microphone was used, as is the practice of Rouch, the French documentary film-maker and pioneer of direct sound. For the other scenes even though several mikes were employed all the mixing was done on the spot.

Similarly, Godard departed from normal cinematic convention towards a more direct approach with his use of colour in **Pierrot le fou**. Colour film stock is very unstable and has to be corrected — the colours made uniform — in the lab after filming. Common practice, dating from the early days of Technicolor, is to use human skin-tone as a basis for this grading. This normally requires heavy red make-up, which is later corrected by adding blue in the lab. However, as Coutard points out (in an article entitled 'Light of Day' from which this and many other of the anecdotes in this section are taken — English translation in *Sight and Sound*, Winter 1965/6): *'with someone like Godard, who has a passion for filming against white walls, everything goes to pieces if the walls turn blue'*.

For the shooting of the film, then, a neutral make-up was used — Coutard again: *'make-up men have their habits, their normal working methods, and it is a crusade to get a more naturalistic kind of make-up out of them.'*

There are a host of similar stories that could be told about the relentless pursuit of 'naturalism' across all the elements of cinematic technology and professional convention. The fundamental question still remains: why this insistence on the technologies and techniques of direct cinema/*cinéma vérité* in the production of film texts which, even in the early stages, are fundamentally anti-naturalistic, which resolutely work against the filmic and pro-filmic codes of the *cinéma vérité* documentary, with its insistence on reality captured on the run, its naive and impossible belief that if you refuse to manipulate the pro-filmic event then the film will capture a reality totally independent of the cinema?

Godard's cinema was thus from the beginning a cinema that combined techniques of direct cinema with a commitment to both montage and *mise en scène*. He thus combined three approaches which were, and to a certain extent are, widely held to be incompatible. André Bazin, the film critic and theoretical mentor of *Cahiers du Cinéma*, had formulated in the late forties an opposition between montage, which was held to interrupt the transparent relation between the film spectator and the object filmed, and a form of *mise en scène*, often exemplified with reference to the Italian neo-realists, which allowed the spectator free access to what was in front of the camera. In an article on montage in 1956, Godard had refused this opposition, arguing that there was never an independent reality which film captured but rather a filmic articulation of reality in which both montage and *mise en scène* had a part to play.

This theoretical break with one opposition was combined with a practical break with the opposition between direct cinema and either montage or *mise en scène*. For practitioners of direct cinema, usually documentary film-makers, montage was anathema, evidencing manipulation of the filmed footage and thus of the spectator (although, of course, editing was grudgingly accepted — twenty-one hours of footage for Rouch's *Chronique d'un été* had to be reduced to a distributable ninety minutes) and *mise en scène* was impossible in that it would constitute manipulation of the object, the pro-filmic event. Godard's careful and precise use of the techniques of direct cinema was in radical contradiction with the ideological aims of direct cinema. The reality he insisted — and insists — on is the reality of the experience of film, and the importance of that reality in the lives of the spectators, not the ability of film to capture reality 'out there' for us 'back here'. For Godard, the technology of direct cinema is used for the investigation of reality through film, not for the negation of the reality of film in that process of investigation.

If the ideologists of direct cinema refused to produce a coherent reality in front of the camera, they nevertheless ignored the coherence produced for that reality by the screen on to which a film is projected. Godard used their techniques to disrupt the coherence of the pro-filmic event but he never forgot the other moment in the cinematic process, a moment ignored by the ideologists of direct cinema, the moment of consumption.

These considerations explain why Godard was eager to criticise Richard Leacock so vehemently in 1963 and yet only a year later was working with Albert Maysles, Leacock's camera operator, for the sketch **Montparnasse-Levallois** which was to appear in the collection *Paris vu par*. About Leacock's 'candid camera' Godard had written:

Leacock is Candide in more ways than one, busily hunting down truth . . . without asking what truth he is after . . . they have no idea what it is they are staging, and that pure reportage does not exist . . . Honesty, in other words, is not enough for a fighter in the avant-garde, particularly when he does not know that if reality is stranger than fiction, the latter returns the compliment. (*Godard on Godard*, pp.202-3).

But Leacock's refusal to order events in front of the camera led to the development of new skills on the part of the cameraman, constantly having to pay attention to everything in the viewfinder. For **Montparnasse-Levallois** the script was written and the actors rehearsed in advance of the shooting with Maysles brought in to film on 16mm, acting **'as a newsreel cameraman, as if he were faced by real events over which he had no control. I tried to organise the happening in the best way possible, but not to direct it like a theatrical production'.**

(*Godard on Godard*, p.212). If much of this attitude to the technology and ideology of direct cinema was implicit in Godard's pre-'68 movies, it was not until he made **Pravda** that the terms of his opposition to the ideology of direct cinema were made explicit.

Pravda was shot in Czechoslovakia in March 1969 ostensibly as a documentary for West German television. Today it can most profitably be seen as a repudiation of contemporary documentary practice rather than as the analysis of Soviet bloc revisionism that it claims to be. Every element of the film's construction denies the possibility of cinematic technology's privileged access to reality.

It is the Dziga-Vertov group's insistence on the primacy of montage which organises the film rather than any notion of a pre-existent reality which finds its correct visual representation. The guiding principle of this montage is analysis but, and here we come to the moment at which the film finally produces a coherence for the spectator, the analysis is always given in advance of any image by the correct political line. The refusal of an ideology of vision in favour of a political analysis is indicated throughout the last section of **Pravda**, when shots of the cameraman reveal that his eyes are not focused on the reality of the pro-filmic event which the camera is bringing back to us from Czechoslovakia but on a copy of Mao's Little Red Book. If finally this dominance of a political analysis is as oppressive as the dominance of vision that it seeks to displace, and there is a voice at the end of the film which suggests this, nevertheless certain steps forward are made in **Pravda**. Above all, the idea that 'seeing is believing', that the camera can illustrate the words of a documentary commentary with images that confirm those words, these founding ideas of film and tele-vision practice are torn apart, dismembered, in **Pravda**.

The first section of the film consists of images of modern Czechoslovakia — images of revisionism, as it were — advertising slogans, old men walking in the streets, young workers, a couple wash-ing their car, shops, televisions and so on. The sound-track contains sync-sound of some of the images as well

From **Pravda**

From **Pravda**

as pop music and sound from television programmes. But this is overlaid with the defining and controlling voice of the commentator, organised as a discourse between Vladimir (Lenin) and Rosa (Luxemburg). This narration is both descriptive: **'Transport for the less fortunate workers'**, **'There are still quite a few small shopkeepers particularly in the large cities'**, and disdainful: **'Many workers would rather wash their cars than fuck their wives'**. This commentary thus supplies us with information which the images themselves are not adequate to supply. It is as if the film has moved away from direct cinema, where sounds and images are deemed capable of 'speaking for themselves', but only to move back towards a more conventional style of television documentary, where the commentator acts as an intermediary between the images and the audience, interpreting them for us, anchoring their ambiguities into one definite meaning to be consumed with ease.

At the end of this section the commentary declares the redundancy and unprofitability of this approach. What emerges is just a **'travelogue'**, which might have been produced by **'Marker or the *New York Times'**. by the left or by the right. Two years previously Godard had contributed a section to the film **Far from Vietnam**, which was made by Chris Marker's production company SLON. Marker's documentary work has been consistent in its commitment to analyse political struggle both in France and abroad: in Cuba, Chile and Vietnam, for example. Yet Godard contributed a section to **Far from Vietnam** in which he talks primarily of his own personal difficulties in making films which resist the 'aesthetic imperialism' of American film-making, but which, at the same time, isolate him from the working class in France. Although those scenes with him at the eye-piece of his Mitchell camera can be easily dismissed as empty solipsism one thing emerges as clear from his investigations at this time and his rejection of the kind of political cinema associated with Marker: the 'evidence of our senses' cannot be trusted and is no

From **Loin du Vietnam**

115

basis for analysis because those senses are always put in place by the common sense of the dominant ideology, that ideology which takes truth as evident and thus ignores our place in that truth. And that place always includes technological determinants so it is of little surprise that Godard, as a film-maker, must include a Mitchell, a product of American technology, in his film about Vietnam. The dominant voice in **Pravda** rejects this evidence of the senses in the following terms: **'It isn't enough because it is only the knowledge perceived by our senses; now we must rise above this perceptive knowledge, we need to struggle to transform it into rational knowledge'.**

The second part of the film announces itself as a **'concrete analysis of a concrete situation'.** We see interviews with students, peasants and industrial workers, but none of these interviews is subtitled or translated. Is this merely an indication that these people do not know what they are saying, that they are victims of some revisionist 'false consciousness', that the film is refusing to allow them to 'speak for themselves'? Or is it, more pertinently, to ask what we would know even if we could interpret these foreign words, to question the basis of any transparent knowledge the film could provide us with? The film stresses our distance from Czechoslovakia ironically when the commentary advises: **'If you don't know Czech you'd better learn it fast'.**

The fact that the dominant relations of sound and image always presuppose that the audience is divorced from their production and the choices made in that production is underlined in the short section that **Pravda** devotes to the Czechoslovak film industry. Overdetermined, as always, by the necessity to construct the 'revisionism' or 'Westernism' of the Czech people, the sound-track to the section is none the less important: **'Here, just as in Hollywood, movies are made for the common man. You go to the people without coming from them. You criticise the people's shortcomings without taking the people's point of view.'**

From **Pravda**

From **Pravda**

As shown in Harold Evans's
Pictures on a Page

From **Pravda**

The commentary accompanies a sequence in which images of workers in a munitions factory making anti-aircraft guns for the North Vietnamese are intercut with images of film workers making sounds and images for popular consumption, the structure of the relation between work and politics in Czechoslovakia entailing that both groups of workers fail to consider either the effects of the work they do or, consequently, their engagement in that work.

This is not without its confusions, or its condescensions, as critics have been swift to point out. But how much more condescending, how much more confused are those films, those photographs, those sounds and images which presume to bring to their audience the true picture of a foreign situation, never considering how the audience that they feel they have every right to speak to is constructed in the organisation of their sounds and images?

The film attempts to resolve these problems in its third section with the dictum, **'to a picture that is sick add a sound that is not sick'**. Such a decision is premissed on the correctness of the sound-track, guaranteed by the correct revolutionary line that Rosa is enunciating. In fact this correctness is hesitantly questioned by Vladimir at the close of the film:

'You say true texts but with what, with images still half-false, you thought we could seize the relations of production between images and sounds just like that, by chance; in fact you've acted dogmatically; what you've ultimately adopted is a lot of posters and slogans. You thought that you'd taken a step forward — result: we've taken two steps backwards.'

Vladimir's intervention carries little weight in the balance of the film and in any case the film ends with a fourth section which finally finds a correct sound, the 'Internationale', to go with the correct revolutionary image: red. What is important from the perspective chosen here is that the relation of correct sound to correct image, even if still held as a possibility, is never considered in the standard terms of film and television documentary. Nowhere is this more evident than in that part of the third section which deals with the peasantry. On the sound-track Rosa spells out the lessons of Lenin's handling of the peasantry. The image that accompanies this analysis is that of two peasants loading a hay cart, an image which constantly changes as the camera zooms in and out. The zoom always functions at the service of an ideology of vision as knowledge in documentary film practice, this ideology operating around metaphors of 'closeness' and 'distance'. Some documentarists, Rouch for one, will never use a zoom, preferring to move closer to the subject being filmed, rather than 'spy' from a distance. In television documentary films the zoom-in generally functions to 'get close' to the subject, to convince the viewer that he can really see what is going on, whilst the zoom-out is characteristically used to 'put the subject in its context', so that the spectator can receive 'a total social picture'. One might also think here of Antonioni's frequent use of the zoom in the films he made in the People's Republic of China, where he would continually zoom in on some small idiosyncratic detail — an old man in a crowd, for example — which questioned the 'total social picture' he was allowed to film, picking out, as it were, the individuality which is lost by looking at the masses. Godard's use here is very different. The zooms themselves are too sudden, calling attention to themselves as technical effects, products of lens technology and functioning differently from the human eye. More significantly as the zoom receives no motivation from the sound-track — Rosa's analysis takes no account of it — it functions to reinforce the fact that the visual image produced by the camera is, in itself, insufficient to give us a picture of reality. Every image already presupposes an articulation with other images and with a sound-track, with an already-understood articulation of reality. But — and this is the question Godard poses — understood by whom? And to what purpose?

In one sense sounds and images are always in contradiction in film — the sound-track running

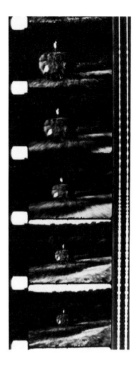

From **Pravda**

118

From **Pravda**

continuously even when nothing is recorded on it, whilst the illusion of movement is achieved by the rapid flickering of still images. For Godard there can be no easy harmonisation of these two technologies in the interests of constructing a world which is readily accessible because easily perceived. If **Pravda** is a film that is continually questioning its own deployment of cinematic technology, that is not necessarily to say that the result is mere confusion. Rather it is truly an 'experimental film', which insists, even at the expense of resolution, that the technology of cinema can never be separated from the way that it is used, from who is using it and from the purpose for which it is being used.

However, **Pravda,** like the other Dziga-Vertov films, never ultimately escapes the assumption that a correct sound-track is possible, that a correct analysis of the situation is available and that, finally, a correct image can complete the ideal film. The granting of primacy to the political meant that both audience and film-maker were defined in political terms. It was not just that the films were made for the politically committed but that politics exhaustively described the situation of the film-maker. When, at the beginning of the second section of **Pravda,** the commentators want to start from their own situation this entails an analysis of the social relations which enabled them to hire the car in which they travel throughout the film. The Maoist slogan to count on one's own forces and its emphasis on the importance of personal struggle amounted to a definition of the personal in terms of the political. It is this exhaustive (exhausting, exhausted) definition which is abandoned in the move away from Paris. The interest in technology does not therefore recede — if anything Godard's interests in questions of cinematic and televisual technology have increased in this period, particularly in video technology. However, the insistence on correctness which under-lined the Dziga-Vertov group's films has been super-seded by questions of subjectivity, which are not just questions of the personal but also questions of the relationship between the subject and information, and the technology required to construct that information.

Two of the episodes from the television programmes on communication, **Six Fois deux,** will serve to illustrate some of the terms in which the tension between questions of the personal and questions of ideology and technology are articulated. The two episodes are **Photos et Cie (Photography and Co)** and **Marcel** and both are specifically concerned with photography. The first episode examines news photography — the public face of the image — whilst **Marcel** examines the work of an amateur film-maker, for whom image-construction is a hobby, an escape from the work he does during the week, work which finances this hobby. But although these programmes deal with other people's work, they are none the less continually concerned with the deployment of technology and the construction of images in the programmes themselves. Contemporary televisual technology offers a range of techniques which provide the possibility of the creation of new relationships between the spectator and the text. Most of these are, of course, systematically repressed in institutional television practice. Just as the technological innovations of the early sixties, marking a new range of possibilities for the articulation of sound and image, quickly became confined, on the whole, to the service of an unproblematic rendering of documentary reality, so the innovations of more recent years in video technology have been confined to, and naturalised by, their use for spectacular reporting of sports events, outside broadcasts and so on. Once again, we see technological innovation not as something with a force, a progress, with its own determining implications, but rather being used to support a particular ideology of the visible. For example, vision-mixing allows for a very simple and rapid way of overlaying one image onto another, or of inserting a smaller image into a portion of the screen. This is used time and again in sports broadcasting, where we see athletes lining up to start a race, with an insert of the starter's gun in the top corner, for example. But it is never used in drama productions, situation comedies

From **Photos et Cie**

From **Nous trois**

They don't want progress.
They want to be first.

From **Photos et Cie**

From **Marcel**

or television fiction generally. Similarly, video technology offers the possibility of writing directly on to the broadcast image, or of punching on captions in a way which is much simpler than film allows, where an optical printing process would be necessary. Again we see this technique in election-night broadcasts, or at the Miss World event, but we never see it used to comment on or to complicate the flow of images in, say, a documentary film or a politician's speech. These are two techniques that Godard has experimented with since **Numéro deux** in order to complicate the relationship between images, sounds and words, and thereby to include the spectator in the construction of the image, to throw the ideology of the visible into crisis. Again television has created the possibility of broadcasting interviews with people, dialogues between people, which could be as long or as short as the situation demanded, but, in the interests of scheduling, ratings and the need to maintain the almost imperceptible flow of television, what we have instead are those short interviews where a television professional patronisingly quizzes a 'member of the public' on how he/she felt when their roof caved in or when their pet goose learned to play the xylophone. These confrontations allow the interviewees no possibility of rephrasing the questions or of taking their own time to answer them. In **Six Fois deux** Godard liberates the television interviews from these constraints — a member of the public, like Marcel, the amateur photographer, or Louison, the dairy farmer, is given as much time to speak as René Thom, the mathematician (in television terms, an expert). The dialogues are conducted without professional spectacularity, or patronisation. So, whilst conducting a theoretical examination of the technological, ideological and economic determinations operating on the images, public and private, which surrounds us, the members of the Sonimage team never hide the technological construction of their own broadcast. It is as if we are seeing television for the first time.

The first section of **Photos et Cie** gives the

audience the opportunity to look for about ten minutes at a news photograph — something which is constructed to make an instant sensational impact before our eyes move on to look at something else. The photograph chosen is of the bayoneting of Biharis accused of collaborating with the Pakistani army. It was taken in Dacca towards the end of the Bangladesh war. It is a typical photograph in many ways, but we should remember that the event recorded was set up as a 'photo-opportunity' to which Western press photographers had been expressly invited. It was an event that had been initiated so that it would be photographed. So we are invited to look closely at this photograph out of its context and for a long period of time — perhaps some might say it is less of an invitation and more of an act of force, but this is a rare opportunity and one which only the cinema or television could achieve as duration is one of the fundamental attributes of those media (though, of course, this is not an attribute that professionals in media are interested in, or rather their sole interest in the time of the image is to deny it — we must change images quickly lest the viewer becomes aware of time). While this photograph is presented to view its photographer delivers a monologue on some of the determinations operating on the construction of such a photograph. Given that the normal context for such a photograph is the newspaper or the news magazine, where it will be looked at only for a few seconds, the task of the professional is to know, intuitively we are led to believe, how to capture that precise five-hundredth of a second which will 'sum up' the event, 'communicating' its 'message' to the reader. As Donald McCullin puts it later in the film, the professional must have '**the knowledge to know which is the right moment . . . to press that button'**; if we have to stop and look at the finished product for very long, if we consider it as a photograph, then it must have failed, it can't have communicated effectively. Once again, of course, every aspect of photographic technology is understood to be at the service of a reality simply waiting to be represented to a spectator.

From **Photos et Cie**

As we watch the Biharis being endlessly bayoneted, the photographer takes us through the technical and economic determinations of the image, determinations which in his discourse are simply part of an immutable and natural order in which his own place is not a subject for interrogation:

'It's a situation you can't control; you can't pose your subjects in photo-journalism, so it comes down to the technical reflexes you have, especially in this type of situation . . . For magazines you've got to deliver the goods. This black-and-white photo might get by in a daily, which doesn't have colour photos. But an Italian or German news magazine often needs colour pictures of an event. So you've got to be able to give them colour as well. But in a case like this one, which you don't control, you can't do that — a flower, yes, I could photograph that calmly in colour and in black and white. In war reporting you can't afford to miss an event with your camera, you've got to catch it. I get it in black and white and forget about the colour. So there, in Dacca, where things were happening fast I used black-and-white Tri-X stock, a very fast film. We were in full sunlight so I set it at a five-hundredth . . . This is the standard speed for capturing abrupt movement. Colour is much more difficult to use because colour film is much slower, so you're working at slower speeds and it's less spontaneous and less sincere than a black-and-white photo, which is faster. Also, in sunlight, you always set the camera between 11 and 16 with a wide-angle lens, a 28mm, so everything is in focus . . . so if anything happens to surprise us we're prepared for it and we try not to be surprised by an action, that's our job.'

As is evident in this monologue, it is impossible to separate the question of the construction of images from the question of their exchange value. It is the image's double position in an economic and ideological circuit of exchange which stimulates the *chasse aux images*, the hunt for images. The specific image from Bangladesh chosen by the Sonimage team was exemplary in this respect in that the various images of this execution became competitors for the Pulitzer Prize, an award which aptly illustrates the articulation of the economic and ideological. Insofar as this articulation is generally recognised it tends to be dealt with in the discourses of humanist morality as a question of individual conscience as, for example, in the editor of the *Sunday Times*, Harold Evans's, comments: '*People were murdered for the camera; and some photographers and a television camera crew departed without taking a picture in the hope that in the absence of cameramen the acts might not be committed. Others felt that the mob was beyond the appeal to mercy. They stayed and won Pulitzer Prizes. Were they right?*' (Evans, 1978, p.xiv).

This moral discourse which refuses to consider the circuits which organise information is very evident in a certain kind of left-wing moralising. Such moralising contents itself with deploring the actual state of the media but considers that nothing more is needed than a change in personnel. This kind of stance refuses to confront the necessary displacements that would interrupt the series of exchanges on which the present organisation of information is founded. There are few better examples of a moralising discourse that refuses to confront problems of subjectivity than that of the French Communist Party. **Photos et Cie** stresses this in the next section of the programme, filmed at a Communist conference at which Georges Marchais, general secretary of the French party, made a speech attacking television reporting. The irony of this is that although Marchais was speaking against the media we see that, in effect, he was speaking for them. In front of the stage from which he delivers his speech are gathered the massed ranks of newsmen from the press, radio and television frantically employed in recording what he says. The members of the public, Marchais's followers, the manual and intellectual workers of France, are confined to the gallery, separated from the speaker by the crowds of professionals below. To whom is the speech addressed? To those who have come to listen or

From **Photos et Cie**

to the newsmen who 'represent' the general public? Always remembering that the very notion of 'general public' is dependent on a particular organisation of information. Over the image of the event Godard writes the following set of polarities, drawing out the contradictions of the event:

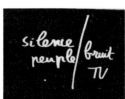

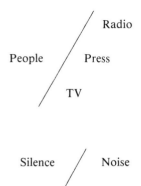

```
                    / Radio
                   /
         People   /  Press
                 /
                /  TV
               /
```

```
                    /
         Silence   /   Noise
                  /
         People   /   TV
                 /
```

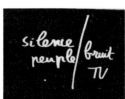

From **Photos et Cie**

and over the direct sound recording of the speech we hear another voice:

'Not producing. Not consuming. Only recording. Just taking stock. Sounds and light produced by others and consumed by others . . . Radio, the press and television. Racing to the four corners of the world. Sticking to events. Getting paid for that. Getting paid for that . . . being a professional for radio, photography and television . . . being a professional.'

The hidden economic and ideological assumptions of photography are elaborated in one of the most striking sequences from the programme, in which Godard sifts through a pile of photographs, talking all the time:

'Professional photographers. There are things you could say but you have to have the time. When you have the time you don't have the space and when you have the space you don't have the time.

'A photo of a tourist who
pays for the right to take photos.
. . . Amateurs pay and professionals don't pay. . . .

That one, yes, she's a model,
must be a professional.

But not that one. . . .

And those, while
they're being searched in prison,
they can get lost if they think they're going to get paid
by the photographer. . .

Vietnam.
How much were all those people paid?
That's the real scandal.
The magazines of the world made a fortune
out of photos from Vietnam.

Captions.
A Chinaman who's shaking hands with Nixon.
The caption reads: "This brave courageous man."
It's the Chinaman who's courageous
shaking the hand of a man like that. . .

126

They always photograph the ones who
are doing the torturing from the back and their
victims face on.

The first photo taken was that of a flower.

The first photo published was of
the gunned- down Communards . . .

A square of paper.
When you look at it closely it's a real landscape
made of paper.
When you look at it close up it smiles . . .

The world is far away,
but television is there, near us, reassuring us'.

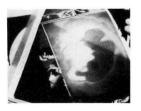

To be able to see you have to turn your eyes.
Open your eyes wide.
To do that you need time,
and you need space. . .'

In the final section of this programme we see, for the first time, news photographs in their context, in the pages of *Le Nouvel Observateur*. But here this context is affirmed in its relation to all the advertisements in the magazine — 'news' and 'information' bolstering up, and being bolstered up, by the demands of commerce. When all the pages containing advertising have been removed, when this literal act of deconstruction has been achieved, there is little else remaining. What does remain cannot stand by itself; news photography demands the context of commodity circulation; it cannot be separated from it.

Marcel makes super-8 movies and 35mm colour transparencies of the flora and fauna of the Alps. His life is engaged in image-making just as much as are those of the professionals in **Photos et Cie,** yet this is seen as a hobby, a 'liberation from everyday work'. As an amateur he pays for this hobby from the money he earns working as a watch-maker. Though the interview with Marcel is anything but a simple illustration of certain theses, and this because of its length and Godard's method of asking questions to which he does not know the answer, it is nevertheless clear that, as an image-maker, he is caught in a circuit of exchange every bit as determining as that in which the professionals labour. These determinations can be read across the whole range of his work — from the type of equipment he uses to the aesthetic decisions he makes and to the places in which and the people to whom his work is exhibited. The contrast between the professionals and someone like Marcel repeats the shifting polarity which runs through **Numéro deux** — that of the *usine* (factory) and *paysage* (landscape), the polarity so central to advanced capitalism in which work and enjoyment are understood as mutually exclusive. To work in our enjoyment, to enjoy in our work, such possibilities are denied in contemporary organisations of space and time. And yet, for Godard, it is only the interfusion of the two that can bring any real satisfaction. Indeed, it is in these terms that one can understand his successive physical displacements

From **Marcel**

From **Marcel**

in the last seven years, as an attempt to base his factory, his studio in the countryside. For Marcel, the factory and the countryside are rigorously separated, although the viewer may find his position at the editing table and his position at his work bench almost identical.

His photographs deliberately concentrate on what is 'beautiful'; this, in effect, means the world of nature; he rarely takes pictures of people. His camera is set on a tripod, his pans are as smooth as can be expected from his super-8 equipment, he focuses clearly on the wild life and wild flowers of the Alps and he has no difficulty at the editing stage of the work in eliminating those images which are 'defective'. Similarly, Marcel seems to keep himself out of his own images as much as possible. He will not speak his own commentaries to his films but relies on music because he feels his speaking voice is not good enough. His ideas about himself, just as much as his use of technology, seems to be coming from another place. However, to dismiss this practice as an aesthetic conservatism would be to miss the point of the broadcast, particularly in its relation to **Photos et Cie.** The Sonimage team may not be setting up Marcel's practice as an escape from the demands of commercial photography, but neither are they concerned to dismiss it. Rather, what are being investigated are the determinations on that practice — the now familiar questions of 'who speaks in an image?' or 'where is the money?' are being asked in relation to another sort of image-making.

These questions are approached, for example, in the following section of dialogue in the film around the differences between stills and movies. It should be noted that the conversation loses some of its force in English because the French word for production line is the same as chain (*la chaîne*) and therefore the emphasis on how one operation necessarily follows another is not as strong in English.

Marcel: **'I can, in still photography, pick up whatever I want. I can go from a tulip to a woman's face; you can't do that in movies.'**

Godard: **'Don't you find you're not so free, then, with movies?'**

'Yes, exactly; with movies I'm less free because I

have to choose a way. It's like writing a book . . . things have to follow on from one another.'

'It's a bit like a production line, then?'

'Yes, a production line — a marvellous production line. The production line of happiness.'

'The production line of what?'

'The production line of happiness.'

'But it's more difficult to follow a production line.'

'Yes, you have to go through every process.'

'And don't you feel imprisoned?'

'Yes, a little imprisoned. The production line is an imprisonment. We have where I work a production line for watches. But it's not the production line of happiness.'

'And don't you think there's something in common between them? All factories have their production lines.'

'Yes.'

'And don't you think there's a similarity between that production line and the fact that in a film there is a production line of images? Perhaps it's the first time you've looked at it like that, but you can try and think about that?'

'Yes, but I'll tell you that perhaps it's not the same production line. The production line is open, deeper, it's the production line you find in nature . . . and from the material, the industrial point of view, I think there's an enormous difference. That's my opinion.'

Not only does this sequence illustrate how Godard's interviews break with normal television patterns but it demonstrates how, for Godard, technical questions immediately engage questions of form: of the relations between the film-maker or film-spectator and the image, relations which cannot be understood by any notion of cinema or photography which would limit them to a series of technical descriptions. It is within this context, ever more stressed since the move towards autonomy and greater control of technological resources signalled by the establishment on Sonimage, that one can understand Godard's collaboration with the Swiss camera-maker, Jean-Pierre Beauviala. Beauviala has constantly attempted to keep his inventions, a product of his radical work in optics, out of the hands of the large corporations and to insist on non-production-line methods of construction. Beauviala is currently producing a 35mm camera, designed to Godard's specifications, which will to a certain extent consolidate the practices that Godard elaborated in the early sixties, combining a Mitchell's quality of image with the size and flexibility of a super-8 camera.

But if the technology of the cinema is an ever more crucial

element in Godard's film-making, that technology has been understood for the last seven years as a technology in which video is perhaps the most important element. Godard's increasing interest in, and use of, video is not to be understood as some final approach to reality, still less as the McLuhanite fantasy of a mechanical extension of the central nervous system which would complete our humanity. Rather the question of the image is now as much a question of video as of film, and specifically of the relation between the two. It is this relation which is one of the focal points of Godard's work since shooting **Numéro deux** on video and then transferring it on to film. **Sauve qui peut** was shot on film but it may be transferred on to video for editing and then transferred back to film. To carry out these complicated operations Godard has finally, after a long struggle, obtained a telecine, a machine which transforms a film image into video and which will enable him to work more directly on both media. The result of that work, the new questions which will silence our answers, must await its use in the editing of **Sauve qui peut** or in some further project.

AATON

Aaton makes J.-L. Godard a 35 mm camera. Ultimate steadiness

Two years ago, the well known film director, J.-L. Godard, commissioned Aaton to make a 35 mm camera. He wanted to combine the advantages of the quantity of information contained in a 35 mm film image, and the ease of handling and unobtrusiveness of super 8 cameras. The first prototype has been in use since April 1979, and the results are more than encouraging.

The Aaton 8-35 is handheld, and has instant magazines; until now, the only 35 mm camera with instant mags has been the Cameflex (1946), which is extremely noisy.

The noise level of the 8-35 is 33 dB. Without any sound absorbing material, the prototype runs at 35 dB; two decibels less is realistic with damping. 33 dB appears quite acceptable in light of the fact that a non-optimum self-blimped 16 mm camera can run in that area.

The steadiness is excellent; it is ensured by the same claw movement system (U.S. patent 3806016) that has made a name for the Aaton 16 mm LTR. The pulldown of the stroke is absolutely linear, with the dead point in the film plane. Willy Lubtchansky, J.-L. Godard's cameraman, contends that the 8-35's steadiness is comparable to that of a Mitchell. On double exposure tests, no visible sign of any movement whatsoever can be observed.

An original feature : a second electric motor in the camera body drives the **60 m and 120 m magazines** through an independant drive clutch.

The 8-35 is **small**, and **light**; it weighs in at around 5 kg. with 60 m mag — slightly less than the Aaton LTR 16 mm camera.

This camera is meant to be a companion to the Panavision or Arri 35 BL : it is easy to handle, unobtrusive, mobile. For certain films, it may even be the only camera ; with a soft blimp, the sound level could be made acceptable for indoor work.

Availability : early 1981.

Price : in the area of 90,000 F with two magazines.

Colin MacCabe:

Could you explain your constant interest in the latest advances in technology?

Jean-Luc Godard;

I usen't be aware of the reason but now I am. It's just because that when it's new it is less rigid, and there are less instructions from the police, the law or circulation. There is not less law, but it hasn't been made, it isn't written down. It is before the written . . . You can handle it, or think you can handle it, which is not the same. You have no rules so you have something to live with, you have to invent some rules and to communicate with other people. 'Are these rules good?' 'Do you think this is a good way to cross a street?' But that's all . . . I was interested because there were no rules. At the time I was attacked and then it became the new mood and I was against it. Because I'm not against that rule, I'm against the fact that it's only that rule, always. I'm not for or against the hand-held camera or sensitive stock. Sometimes you need a hand-held camera, sometimes you need a steady one. I'm against always being obliged to use just one. As soon as there is something new there is less law and then you discover that there are very few people who are interested in working with you because they are lost. You have to find rules in yourself and when to work more or to love. Remember, I was condemned and condemned to make pictures with small money. Why? I could use a lot of money but then you'd be condemned to only make big pictures.

Why have you always used very small crews?

Sometimes because I liked it but sometimes I was obliged to. When you have huge crews it's like going to a city. You know no one. You're not obliged to talk. People discover that it's much more difficult to work with me in a small crew because if you're trying to work differently then you're just obliged to invest. You're not just a hired professional who can escape. If you're a father then the director has a right to speak to you about being a father if the film you're making is about childhood. You can ask your camera operator, 'What do you think as a father' — and then the operator discovers that he doesn't like me because the question is too rough. But if you have a huge crew you never know, you just say 'Hello', 'How are you?', 'Wonderful'. The fact is that I don't make any distinction between reality and the image of it. That's what you must understand. A scientist, a physicist is only a physicist when he studies, when he's working on physics, not when he's at home. I see no difference between reality and an image of reality. For me they're the same. I always say, 'A picture is life and life is a picture'. And when I make pictures, it's making life and that's why it's very hard for the crew to follow and that's why I prefer to keep them small. Because at least, even if we don't talk, even if there's no relationship, at least they can follow. If there were a hundred, well, the picture would never get done.

OK. You say there's no difference between the real and the image. At the same time, before you make your image, you have a fantastic commitment to the real. On the *Hornuss* field, for example, ★ you could have tried to synchronise an interesting bit of the game, a train passing and the dialogue. But if it didn't happen, you wouldn't make it happen.

★ For a description of Godard's direction at the game of *Hornuss*, see Chapter 2, pp.43-44.

I'm trying to make music in the country. If I go to the woods to make good music, a music inspired by the wood or the animals and then shoot every animal and chop down every tree so that I was sure I was making my own music . . . well, it's the same with the film.

I'd still like to understand better the basis of the commitment to the real. The fact that you wouldn't direct . . .

But I'm directing a direction. I don't see. There's no difference between shooting and the following of something when the camera isn't turning. That's something which people in the movies don't understand. Something that is interesting about video is that the camera is always running. The tape-recorder is not running, not always. Of course, in television they only use that for live shows. But for me it's always running. To shoot is to re-run. But before, when I'm going to shoot, I'm not sure. A novelist doesn't think that the only time he's writing a novel is when he's sitting at a table writing. Or a painter or a musician. It's an attitude you only find in the movies and that's incredible or just silly. I prefer to say 'silly' to people because they are angry when you say that but if you said 'incredible' they wouldn't react at all.

Could you give the chronology of your interest in video?

I can't really remember . . . I remember when I tried to use one of the first video outfits made by Philips in '67 in *La Chinoise*. I wanted the characters to shoot themselves and then use the footage for self-criticism but it was too new as equipment then . . . I don't know why I got interested. Maybe because it wasn't run by movie people so there was no law. It was movie equipment and there was no law. So I was authorised. Even with a camera, a Pentax or a Nikon, there are so many people who'll say, 'if you're out of focus, that's no good'. So you hesitate to use it because you think, 'I'm not able to'. Just like Anne-Marie often says about movies. And I say, 'Just by saying that you prove that you are able'. It's very hard to convince people. Of course there is skilfulness in a lot of areas but the whole process should be more accessible. I don't know what the rules were in England but when I began to make movies in France only the camera-operator and the director were authorised to look in the viewfinder. The other members of the crew couldn't. It was like the Middle Ages. Everybody had a category.

133

So the interest in video grew out of the fact that it was cheaper and that there were less rules?

Yes, maybe. Maybe too because you have the whole system. You have a theatre which is the TV set. You have a laboratory which is the tape-recorder. At any time you can always make a picture. I can always borrow, or kill someone. You just need small money, you don't have to beg from a banker. So at least I feel secure. Possibly it's like a hunter who has a bow and arrow. Yes, there are cannons but the bow works all the same. I think there is something in that. I've never done it that way. But I always say, 'if I lose everything I can still go on now, more than ever'. If movie-makers say they can't make a film, I say, 'that's not true, you can make a picture'. There's slides, there's small cassette recorders, like the one we're using now. When I started the tape-recorder took up half the room. It's not true. You can record a sound and if nobody's interested in buying then the only one to blame, maybe not the only one but the most important one, is yourself.

I've been particularly struck by the lighting in your video programmes. Could you say what principles you use in lighting?

I wish I could be . . . That's why I was interested in video too, because at least you can look at the lighting and begin to free yourself from the photographer as the sorcerer who knows the magic that you don't know. He knows what's in the black box and all you know is that he takes it away and four days later he brings it back. But at least in video you can say, 'It's dreadful' or 'It's beautiful, I like it that way'. And then he says, 'You like this dreadful thing?' and you say, 'Yes' and you can learn, can begin to learn but then it means sharing the whole equipment and all the social things. And that's why most of the time I don't light. I don't light because at least there is no rule; there is only one rule: to try to get the right aperture. And then you discover that there is a whole world of difference between 2.2 and 5.6 and the operator doesn't know why he's choosing one world rather than another. They hope there's a reason and I try to work on that reason but *before* the shooting and then they don't want to work, they just want to do their job. Or if they're famous for opening at 5.6 then they're like Steve McQueen. He's paid five million dollars and then he acts in a certain way but you can't ask him to do something for five million dollars. The more he's paid, the less you can ask. Just like a king.

Although colour's very important in your work, I couldn't find any way to talk about it. It's like a difficulty that I have with Joyce's *Finnegans Wake*. The most complex, difficult part of the book is about the children's discovery of colour and how that's related to sexuality and to shame. I'm convinced there's something there but I can't say it.

134

One can't say it . . . It's fifty years since I read books like Joyce or Céline. But I think that in a movie something can be done, that you can mix things like Joyce but in a normal way and more accessible too, not difficult because to look is not something uneasy.

From *Finnegans Wake*

ning. Fools top! Singty, sangty, meekly loose, defendy nous from prowlabouts. Make a shine on the curst. Emen.

But the duvlin sulph was in Glugger, that lost-to-lurning. Punct. He was sbuffing and sputing, tussing like anisine, whipping his eyesoult and gnatsching his teats over the brividies from existers and the outher liubbocks of life. He halth kelchy chosen a clayblade and makes prayses to his three of clubs. To part from these, my corsets, is into overlusting fear. Acts of feet, hoof and jarrety: athletes longfoot. Djowl, uphere!

Aminxt that nombre of evelings, but how pierceful in their sojestiveness were those first girly stirs, with zitterings of flight released and twinglings of twitchbells in rondel after, with waverings that made shimmershake rather naightily all the duskcended airs and shylit beaconings from shehind hims back. Sammy, call on. Mirrylamb, she was shuffering all the diseasinesses of the unherd of. Mary Louisan Shousapinas! If Arck could no more salve his agnols from the wiles of willy wooly woolf! If all the airish signics of her dipandump helpabit from an Father Hogam till the Mutther Masons could not that Glugg to catch her by the calour of her brideness! Not Rose, Sevilla nor Citronelle; not Esmeralde, Pervinca nor Indra; not Viola even nor all of them four themes over. But, the monthage stick in the melmelode jawr, I am (twintomine) all thees thing. Up tighty in the front, down again on the loose, drim and drumming on her back and a pop from her whistle. What is that, O holytroopers? Isot givin yoe?

Up he stulpled, glee you gees, with search a fling did die near sea, beamy owen and calmy hugh and if you what you my call for me I will wishyoumaycull for you.

And they are met, face a facing. They are set, force to force. And no such Copenhague-Marengo was less so fated for a fall

135

From **Sauve qui peut**

6:
TELEVISION.

If I'm making movies it's only because it's
impossible to make TV, because it's ruled by governments everywhere.
Godard, *The Listener* 12 December 1968

My ideas only get through on television.
Godard, *Pariscope* 24-30 September 1975

Unlike many film-makers, Godard has never regarded television as an inferior version of film. Early in his career he expressed his desire to work in television and it has been a recurrent theme in his interviews since 1964. And, indeed, Godard's financial connection with television has become of the utmost importance since 1968. All but one of the Dziga-Vertov films were financed by television and Sonimage has received its major commissions from French and Mozambique television. But if Godard regards television as important, he does not, as so many do, regard it as the same medium as film. Indeed his insistence on the importance of institutions and technology prevents any acceptance of the notion of a 'medium of communication'. If the matters of expression, sound and image, are common to film and television, the institutions and technology, the forms and the audience are very different. When Godard said he wanted to work for television, he did not mean that he wanted to make films for television; his ambition was to work on news and sport.

Television is endlessly debated but little understood. Indeed Godard's own programmes reveal how primitive our thinking about television is. Almost all debate about television circles round its possible or potential 'effects'. 'Does it promote violence?' 'Does it discourage literacy?' These and many other questions are always couched in terms of an individual in whom the 'effects' of television can be measured. Psychology, the science of a ruling class determined to examine the individual in all his or her multitudinous facets, is called to understand a new activity, the watching of television. And the premiss of the investigation is that the activity is discrete, separable and separate from the other practices that constitute our lives.

In contradiction with this position two emphases, both of which run through Godard's theory and practice, need to be made. On the one hand, it is only possible to consider television within the wider economic and ideological divisions of labour in our society. On the other, it is necessary to investigate, rather than take for granted, the forms of visibility that television offers. There is a particularly clear statement of how these emphases affect one's conception of television in a short document that Sonimage produced for the Mozambique government. This document was divided into four sections: the current situation, principles for reflection, possible work and financial aspects. The first two sections provide one of the clearest statements of Godard's thinking on television and provide the terms in which to discuss his own programmes:

Current situation

In general, a country which goes in for television (after first going in for radio particularly) begins by equipping itself with one or several transmitters (stations) from which

it sprays / arroser

or

it floods / inonder

the territory that it declares its own. And as it doesn't have its own programmes, it goes into debt culturally and financially to neighbours, close or distant, who already possess the same system of spraying or flooding.

And as it has already gone into debt to buy the technical equipment (cf. Télé/Zaire), it is thus a double cultural and financial debt that it takes on, accumulating in this way a parasitic capital which will, sooner or later, shatter its hopes of independence (like a delayed action mine or virus — so true is it that communications (l'information) in general has in particular something to do with cancer).

The questions which a television and cinema enterprise like Sonimage asks itself are the following:

'Before sending out an image, perhaps we should ask what image, or an image of what?'

'Before appointing a minister of posts, perhaps we should ask if one needs or wants to write a letter, and to whom and why (to do what) and against what?'

And if time sometimes equals money, the speed or slowness with which one replies to these questions are each worth different amounts of money.

Sonimage does not claim to be anything more than a workshop in which one can pose onseself these problems in a practical fashion (un tapis où l'on peut se poser pratiquement ces problèmes).

Principles of reflection

A. in a cinema

people are many ★ (together)

to be alone ★ in front of the screen.

★ Godard's document talks of the difference between *plusieurs* and *seul*. I have translated *plusieurs* as *many* throughout and *seul* either as *alone* or as *one (alone)*.

B. in an apartment linked to a TV aerial

people are alone to be many (together)

in front of the screen

that's to say:

set A: many to be (become) alone (cinema)

set B: alone to be (become) many (TV)

139

that's to say:

$$A = \text{many} \longrightarrow \text{one (alone)}$$
$$B = \text{one (alone)} \longrightarrow \text{many}$$

that's to say:

journey out (aller)   { from cinema to TV }   or   { from A to B }   or   { from many to one (alone) }

return (retour)   { from TV to cinema }   or   { from B to A }   or   { from one (alone) to many }

thus the following schema:

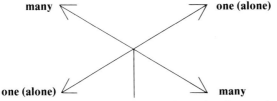

many   ↗↙   one (alone)

one (alone)   ↙↘   many

Sonimage is situated at the crossing between the departure and the arrival of information.

Sonimage is a manufacturer of light in the sense of throwing light on a situation to see it clearly or, on the contrary, to draw the veil.

Godard's estimate of the current situation stresses how television finds its place not as an isolated element within the individual's life but as part of a complex of social developments which involves not only the development of economic relations capable of producing a commodity as technologically complex as television but also the concomitant social changes which make television an appropriate form of entertainment★. Crucial in these developments, and crucial to Godard's concerns, is the ever increasing division of labour in a developed capitalist economy, a division of labour which cannot be understood only in terms of economic development for it includes wider patterns of living: most crucially, the potentially mobile nuclear family and the forms of accommodation and entertainment that accompany it.

★ Perhaps the only book which fully addresses these problems is Raymond Williams's *Television: Technology and Cultural Form* (1974), the first two chapters of which contain a penetrating analysis of television's place in a developed capitalist economy.

It is to this family that television is addressed in forms which do not exist in the cinema. To watch a film is to go out of the home and be entertained as an individual. To watch television is to stay at home and be entertained as a member of a national public. This is the point of Godard's distinction between the one and the many and it points to a crucial difference in the organisation of sound and image. In cinema it is the articulation of narrative and vision which positions the individual spectator, in television it is direct address which established the spectator as part of a national audience and holds the variety of programmes in place★. It is the importance of the announcements, of the placing of programmes within a general pattern of entertainment which holds the variety of sound and image in place. Any evening's entertainment will include fiction, news, documentary, etc. Each of these organises sound and image in specific ways but they are securely located within a pattern of an evening's viewing. The whole functioning of television is to produce a world visible and comprehensible at the touch of a switch and in whose production no other effort is required. If a film on television might make different claims (the images will become visible only on condition that we follow a narrative), those claims are subordinated to the announcer and to the announcer's supports in the television magazines and the television pages of the press. Given this dominance of direct address in television and its control of the image, it is perhaps not surprising that Godard's television programmes are almost totally without direct address, although there is a great variety of forms used within each programme. If Godard wishes to comment on an image, he uses the possibilities of vision-mixing to write directly on the screen thus producing a comment whose relation to the image is not authorised by the form.

★ I am indebted to Stephen Heath and Gillian Skirrow's article 'Television: a world in action' (1977) for my understanding of the importance of direct address. Many of my other comments on the functioning of Godard's television are similarly indebted.

Although many of the Dziga-Vertov films were made for television, they were made as films with little, if any, concern for their possible transmission on television. The work with video that started with the setting up of Sonimage obviously prepared Godard for a greater interest in television. This interest achieved some possibility of realisation with Giscard d'Estaing's election in 1974. Committed to a series of cosmetic liberal reforms of the authoritarian Gaullist state, one of Giscard's first actions was to break up the ORTF, the organisation that controlled French broadcasting into a series of semi-autonomous units. It was one of these, INA (the national institute of audiovisual art), that was to co-produce two series of television programmes with Sonimage. The first, **Six Fois deux (Sur et sous la communication) Six Times Two (On and Under Communication)** was, as its title indicates, six programmes each composed of two units of 50 minutes each. It was made in Grenoble in 1975 and 1976 and was shown on the third channel in France on six successive Sundays in the late summer of 1976. The second commission, **France/tour/détour/deux/enfants (France/Tour/Detour/Two/ Children)** was made in Paris and Rolle in 1978 and is made up of twelve half-hour programmes which were intended to be shown daily over a two week period by the second channel. At the time of writing these programmes have yet to be broadcast and, if they are, they are unlikely to be shown daily but rather in four blocks of three in a slot reserved for films by great directors ★.

The two units of the third programme of **Six Fois deux, Photos et Cie** and **Marcel,** have already been discussed in the previous chapter and the relation between the two units is typical of all six. The first section examines a problem theoretically and conceptually and the second, in the form of an interview, holds some of the concerns of the first half in

★ Godard's television programmes have only been shown at special events in Great Britain. However, the British Film Institute has now obtained British rights for both series of programmes and they should soon be available for general distribution in English versions.

tension with the particular experience of an individual life. The first programme considered problems of work: **Y a personne (Nobody's There)** deals with urban unemployment and attitudes to work while in **Louison** a French peasant talks of the overwork in the country which complements the lack of employment in the towns. The second addresses itself to problems of signification, particularly in relation to the image. **Leçons de choses (Lessons about Things)** takes its title from a division in French kindergarten between 'lessons about things' *(leçons de choses)* and 'lessons about words' *(leçons de mots)* but the strategy of the programme was to cast the validity of such a distinction in doubt; indicating how it was impossible to identify things outside a system of meaning, a system with its specific production and distribution in which one was allotted a particular place. Its insistent message was that no image could be understood outside the particular conditions of its production and reception. Its repeated question was **'Where and when do you find yourself there?'**. It was this question that must be posed to the image, a question which related the image to one's own life and experience. The repetition and strangeness of this question brings home the extent to which the whole contemporary operation of sound and image is devoted to erasing that life and experience in favour of an image which appears with its own guarantee of interest and appropriateness. This investigation was followed by the interview **Jean-Luc**, in which Godard was questioned by two journalists from the French radical daily *Libération*. The third programme considered photography in **Photos et Cie** and **Marcel★**. The fourth programme was entitled **Pas d'histoire (No History)** and **Nanas.** Both titles need some explanation. The

★ For an analysis of **Photos et Cie** and **Marcel** see above pp.120-130.

phrase *pas d'histoire* can be understood either as an indicative, *no history/no story,* or as a colloquial imperative, *Don't make a fuss.* The programme tries to understand the relation between 'fuss' and narration and then to understand that in four women's accounts of their lives. It is they who make up the contributors to **Nanas;** the title is a generic term for women which is most adequately translated as *Birds.* This episode is much the least satisfactory of all six, as Miéville states at the end of **Nanas** when she pours scorn on Godard's attempts to say something about women. Neither half of the programme succeeds in doing more than stating rather than proving relationships. Indeed for some time Sonimage would not send out copies of this fourth programme, although they have now changed their mind.

From **Nous trois**

From **René(e)s**

The fifth programme is entitled **Nous trois (Us Three)** and **René(e)s.** The first half is entirely without spoken dialogue. A man in prison writes an endless letter, reproduced on the screen, to his lover. Their faces are juxtaposed on the screen in a frenzy of vision-mixing as Godard attempts to understand in terms of video a mystery whose explanation is endlessly sought in the films: how from a relationship in which there are only two terms is a third term with a life of its own, the relation itself, produced? Godard reflects on this paradox at a variety of levels from the most evidently material, the birth of a child, to the most rigorously formal. It is the interest in formalism, an interest that Godard claims to date from his earliest years, which led Godard to interview the mathematician René Thom about his catastrophe theory, and how he understood the relations between mathematics and life. But Thom's grinning common-sense in which mathematics simply offers another way of stating the most banal truisms rather than offering new explanations, evidently offended Godard, for Thom is not treated with the sympathy accorded to the other interviewees. Indeed while Godard had commented on Louison's rush of speech with the written admonition to viewers that, although they might have had enough, Louison should be listened to as he spoke true **(il dit vrai),** Thom's comments are frequently overlaid with the brief written comment: **'false'.** The final programme opens with a retrospective of the whole series, a consideration of the project of **'doing television differently'**, which is entitled **Avant at après (Before and After).** This is followed by **Jacqueline et Ludovic** in which Godard talks to two people who communicate 'differently': Ludovic, who can only string together sets of idiomatic connecting phrases, and Jacqueline, who talks fluently about her attempts to marry Pope Paul VI.

The lack of direct address in the programmes is emphasised in **Avant et après.** The single speaker's consideration of the series is not delivered to camera but to an invisible interlocutor

From **Avant et Après**

with a hesitation and idiomatic quality to the speech emphasised when the programme 'quotes' a section of ordinary continuity from a standard evening's viewing. There are three further elements which sharply distinguish these programmes from the television that we are used to watching. The first, and probably the most immediately striking, is the amount of footage shot from a fixed camera position. The inferior quality of the image in television puts even more emphasis on holding attention through constant change of shot. Normal television works on frequent cutting from one shot to another in such a way that space is comfortably articulated but that articulation never jars because of the continual change from one point of view to another, all guaranteed by and guaranteeing the relation of vision, all constructed by and constructing a visible world. In the Sonimage programmes the camera rarely moves and, if it does, there is a deliberation to its movement that draws attention to what is seen as the product of a particular choice rather than an ineluctable epiphany. In particular, the interviews are shot from one position without any of the usual shot/reverse shots which establish the interviewee and the interviewer in the same place at which we, the viewers, look. The effect of this dislocation is to place the interviewer and viewer in the same indeterminate place from which their relation to the interview must be constructed. **'When and where do you find yourself there?'** The question forces itself upon us.

An announcer welcomes the viewer to an evening's entertainment.
Quoted in **Avant et après**

   The second very evident change in relation to normal television is the selection of images. The whole organisation of television assumes that there are professionals who can select our images for us. The political struggles for free speech over the last three hundred years mean that there is a general awareness that people have the right to use their own words, although that still leaves open the question of what it is to speak for oneself. But the existence of television professionals denies that there is any question of whether we should be able to use our own images, let

144

★ When in the interview with René Thom, images are used to punctuate the mathematician's words, it is evident that they are not *his* images nor some neutral illustration but material provided by Sonimage to work against his words.

From **Louison**

alone the further problem of what it would be to see for ourselves. One of the emphases of the first three programmes is how odd people find the request to provide images to express their thoughts or positions: that is the job of television professionals, of skilled communicators, is the implied response. But it is a job that Godard and the Sonimage team refuse to take on ★. If Louison cannot provide images to accompany what he is saying, so be it. Louison talks directly to camera for nearly an hour and, apart from that and his arrival at the site of the interview in a tractor, the only image provided is of him bringing his cows in to be milked, an image shot from the road; the view of an outsider. The political question of who has the right to use images poses itself insistently in Godard's texts. And such a question is not without its implications for the position of the viewer. The assumption that any work on the image is the specialised job of professionals shatters at every turn in **Six Fois deux.**

The third striking feature of the television programmes is the selection of people to be interviewed. It is not simply that, with the exception of Thom and Godard himself, they are people with none of that inevitability which fame and success confer. It is, after all, a standard strategy of television documentary to consider the lives of 'ordinary' people. But such considerations are normally rigorously determined in advance. We will look at that couple because they are typical of the upper-middle income bracket, we will look at this adolescent in order to understand changing attitudes to violence. In every case the individual represents a type, understood in relation to an agreed image of society. Godard's interviewees are very different. The crucial factor in their selection is not their typicality but their willingness to consider questions to which neither they nor the interviewer (Godard) already know the answer. This is made evident in **Y a personne** when a selection of unemployed people answer an advertisement for a job that Sonimage had placed at the local labour exchange. The job is simply to be interviewed by Godard about their attitudes to work. However, only two of those interviewed are willing to continue the interview past the stage where the answers are known in advance. The determining feature of these interviews is not the *representation* of positions but the joint exploration of a problem, itself not fully defined in advance. This method of interviewing places great strains on the viewer. He or she must be equally willing to participate or else they will simply lapse into boredom.

The radical demand that Godard addresses to the viewer is to actively participate in the production of meaning. The emphasis is always on a joint exploration, on the dissolution of an object under investigation, the interviewee, and a subject who investigates, the interviewer acting as the representative of the viewer. For Godard we only communicate at the moment when we, too, are listening to what we say, when we listen to ourselves to understand the message being produced. It is only at the moment that we pay attention to our position as a viewer, of 'where and when we find ourselves there', that any communication can take place. This view of communication is spelt out in **Leçons de choses** when Godard analyses the behaviour of the sailors from the battleship *Potemkin* in Odessa in 1905. What is important for Godard is that when the sailors went into the town to bury one of their comrades, they didn't know in advance what they were doing. That they were demonstrating is true but Godard insists that their demonstration cannot be understood in terms of the contemporary fixed political form. They were attempting to show people something, to indicate what they had done on their ship. They were demonstrating, not going on a demonstration. The emphasis in Godard's analysis is that the communicating subject's own ignorance of what is being said is a crucial factor in any real act of communication ★.

Godard's example of a stereotyped form which is incapable of communication is the contemporary political demonstration. Because everybody knows exactly what is being expressed, nothing is communicated. Godard's expositions of communication and politics are inseparable and make clear the critique to which he lays himself open. The privileging of moments of radical change, of a communication ★ Godard's theory of communication is thus directly opposed to a communications theory which holds to a model of sender, receiver, message and channel. There is no message independent of the relation between sender and receiver and that relation is not understood in terms of some neutral channel but rather as a complex which cannot be analysed into three separate component elements.

which displaces the subject into a new identity, ignores the necessary struggles and pleasures of stereotype. Demonstrations are not just methods to communicate new states of being, they are also one of a number of methods of affecting and inflecting the political process. The recent attempts to reverse the advances of the Abortion Act of 1967 have been largely stopped by the mobilisation of people in demonstrations and petitions. Godard's arguments that these forms are stereotyped seem a short step from the abandonment of the whole ground of political struggle.

And this political critique can be extended further to Godard's work, or more specifically, to the discourses with which this book has attempted to argue in favour of Godard's work. The emphasis throughout this book has been on the way in which the institutions of 'communication and entertainment', film and television, entertain by erasing, give pleasure in exchange for being, hide their own work so that the spectator can relax. Crucial to the thrust of Godard's work and to this book's exposition is an unmaking of the snares of identification operated by systems of signification in which production and consumption are rigorously divorced. But there is a point at which the discourse stops, where the argument comes to an end in a series of choices which are more

146

complicated. The pleasures of identification are not so easily denied nor can they be simply rejected. What this book has done is to argue for Godard's work in film and television, for the knowledge and desire that they incite. So to do is inevitably to ignore the problem, less banal than it might appear, of boredom.

Finally, the lessons we learn from Godard's work presuppose a different system of distribution: film and television which would no longer be relayed through financial, administrative and technical centres but which would be distributed amongst producers. Such a distribution system shows little sign of being constructed and in its absence Godard's work rests on the contradiction that we can be interested in it only in so far as we are interested in Godard.

In **Avant et après** when members of the Sonimage team consider what has been accomplished in the first series of television programmes, they reflect on the paradox that in order to show their work to neighbours in Grenoble, they have had to pass through Paris, through the centre. To indicate what a local TV might be (in **France/tour/détour/deux/enfants** frequent reference is made to the fact that the programme is not part of national TV but a TV of the 15th *arrondissement* in Paris) one has to appear on national TV. The turning point of this contradiction is Godard's own name. It is because of his fame, constructed by the traditional relations of production and consumption, that Sonimage's work is possible. And it is within a centrally organised system that it finds its distribution ★ . It is true that the programmes themselves work against that system in that they demand an interest that is not simply provided by vision, by an agreed image of a national audience, but is the product of a specific work on sound and image. We follow the dialogues between Godard and Louison, or Marcel, as active participants. But the basis for that activity can only (apart from those who know Louison or Marcel or are actively engaged in similar practices) be our interest in Godard's continuing work, in a commitment to the particular project on which he is engaged. When the Sonimage team consider this problem in **Avant et après,** they attempt to explain it in terms of the **'fraud' (escroquerie)** on which the whole television system is based and in which Godard's name is simply another fraudulent moment.

★ It is an added complication that there is a real sense in which French television refused to distribute them. **Six Fois deux** was put out on the minority third channel and most of it was broadcast in August at the height of the holiday season. **France/tour/détour/deux/ enfants** is unlikely to receive the regular half-hour spot for which it was intended. Instead it will be presented as the work of a famous film-maker.

This answer is, however, ingenuous. It ignores both the conditions under which such work could be more generally engaged in and the problem of the viewer who has none of that commitment to Godard which is a pre-supposition of the attention necessary to avoid boredom. Godard confronts this problem directly in the eleventh episode of **France/tour/détour/deux/enfants.** This series of programmes differs considerably from the first. Considerably shorter at half an hour, each episode has a similar structure, generating some of that repetition which is so general in television. These two considerations, length and structure, mean that **France/tour/détour/deux/enfants** resembles conventional television programmes more than **Six Fois deux**. At the same time the heterogeneity of the material used and the refusal to order it finally for the viewer breaks with the dominant forms of television.

The opening credits sequence of each programme shows two young children, a girl (Camille Virolleaud) and a boy (Arnaud Martin) in a television studio, handling microphones and camera. These images are accompanied by a soundtrack of popular music. The only variation in this sequence is that whichever child is to be the 'subject' of the programme handles the microphone, leaving the camera to the other. The opening sequence of each programme observes one of the children engaged in a routine daily task: undressing for bed, going to school, eating supper and so on. These opening shots constantly move in and out of slow motion, attempting, as the spoken commentary emphasises, to de-compose these ordinary movements so that we can see what is at stake in our most routine tasks. The reflections prompted by this sequence serve as an introduction to the next brief section in which the themes of each programme (spelt out in block capitals on the screen) are introduced. The first programme started with shots of Camille undressing for bed and then went onto considerations of obscurity and chemistry, the processes by which we start a night or a television programme. The next section is introduced with and punctuated by the caption **VERITE (TRUTH)**. In the majority of programmes Godard talks to one of the children about the themes of the programme. In some, however, we see them participating (or not) in one of the series of verbal exchanges in which they are addressed in the school or with their family. In both cases the camera frames the child in close-up and we never see Godard or their other interlocutors. This material, which composes most of each programme, is commented on in voice-over and in a sequence entitled **TELEVISION** by the adult protagonists: Betty Berr and Albert Dray. The end of the children's contribution is announced by the only moment of direct address in Godard's television when

From the first episode of
France/tour/détour/deux/enfants

★ The French word *histoire* means both *history* and *story*. Often Godard's use of this word can only be understood if both meanings are borne in mind.

a sequence entitled **HISTOIRE (STORY)** ★ is introduced by one of the two adults. The 'directness' of this address is both emphasised and undercut. Emphasised by the colloquialness and hesitancy of the speaker; undercut by the fact that in each of the twelve programmes exactly the same hesitant speech is delivered (except for the changes of gender determined by which child has just been talking): **'And I think that — I think now that — we need a story, and not her** own **story, not a story that would come from her but she would come from a story . . . and both . . . but both** before: **she before and the story after, the story before and her after . . . above and below.'**

It is this story which then follows in a short sequence of images and sounds which are finally commented in another sequence entitled **TELEVISION** which ends with the promise of another story.

The complexity of material in these programmes is astounding: to do them justice would require another book. The aim is not to produce the truth of our society by an appeal to an innocence unsullied by our fallen world; the children provide the detour which allows the Sonimage team to pose certain questions about the contemporary world. In the first programme Godard's questioning of the child is interrupted by the voice of Betty Berr which states: **'he doesn't want to obtain an image or a sound but the passage of a signal'.** What the children say is given the caption **TRUTH** but this truth is not one which provides the explanation for the rest of the programme; it simply provides the raw material which is commented on by **TELEVISION** and contrasted with **STORY**. Indeed, to continue with the first episode as example, it is evident that Camille has little conscious idea of obscurity; it is only clarity for which she can find examples and to which she can relate her life. It is the detour of the question, the traverse of the signal, that enables the **STORY** to take place. Camille's inability to think about obscurity gives extra force to the unrolling of the **STORY**: a consideration of the most obscure chemistry, the most mysterious beginning of all: the birth of a

From the first episode of
France/tour/détour/deux/enfants

149

child. The process by which two becomes three and how this generation also spells death is examined in an image of quite extraordinary force: a pregnant woman has superimposed on her stomach an ever-growing image of a baby, one that finally blots her out altogether. If this inventive use of the technological resources of television gives us an example of how Godard enables us to see anew, there can be no question but that the failure to pay the closest attention to the progression of the images, to the inflection of the sound will result in an immediate lapse into boredom. Without the closest attention the images become alternately too static and too frenetic, too slow and too fast — there is no question of a simple point of view that we can adopt.

From the 11th episode of
France/tour/détour/deux/enfants

From the first episode of
France/tour/détour/deux/enfants

The political and aesthetic problems of this practice are made absolutely evident in the penultimate programme of the series. The introductory slow motion sequence shows Camille setting the table for supper while the commentary asks what the relations are between the family and larger social units. The sequence which suggests the themes of the progamme opens with an extraordinary zoom shot that moves from a conventional image of natural beauty to reveal the smoke-belching factory nestling in the mountains around the lake we have been admiring. This shot is followed by the captions: **TOUS (ALL)**, **REALITE (REALITY)** and **LOGIQUE (LOGIC)** which introduces a

series of shots of a set of dice being rolled as the commentary spells out the unthinkable number of calculations necessary to specify the various biological possibilities that make up one human body. These considerations lead to the conclusion that it is the complexity of the physiological processes involved in reproduction which have led the monsters ★ to their two most important inventions: a sexuality which exceeds and cannot be reduced to the physiology of reproduction and a death which has nothing to do with the external possibilities of physical annihilation but is a sentence imposed from within. These conclusions are accompanied by an extraordinary montage of images of sex and destruction culled from pornographic and news magazines.

★ Throughout **France/tour/ détour/ deux/enfants** adult humans are referred to as 'the monsters'.

From the 11th episode of
France/tour/détour/deux/enfants

The section entitled **TRUTH** frames Camille as she eats with her parents and younger brother, listening and occasionally participating in the family conversation. The scene recalls the image of a hand scooping soup from a bowl in **Lotte in Italia.** The visual difference is that we now see the face to which the hand is delivering soup and the result is a very different

emphasis from that of **Lotte in Italia.** In the earlier film the image was a visual element that could not be comprehended outside the ideological structures that produce the family. It was only work on the sound, on the analysis of ideology, that could give an image meaning. **France/tour/détour/deux/enfants** grants a new primacy to the image. What we see is that in our accorded places we are not visible. Unable to follow visually the conversational logic that her family is engaging in, we are forced to concentrate on Camille, on her invisibility within the family, on the fact that nobody but us is looking at her. If we see Camille reacting to the conversation — to her father's questions about school or her parents' laughter at her younger brother's pronouncements that he doesn't want to sleep with ladies (*dames*) but only with fathers — we are also aware that these reactions are not registered by the family, caught up in the routine of a family supper.

From the 11th episode of
France/tour/détour/deux/enfants

Dray's and Berr's comments on this sequence spell out the consequences and problems of Godard's and Sonimage's project. Berr complains that the audience is going to be bored by the length of the scene. Dray objects that as the audience is engaged in family meals all day long it is impossible for the scene to be too long for them. Berr replies that it is precisely because it is what the audience does all day long that renders it unsuitable for television. This answer allows Dray to repeat an emphasis which runs through all the programmes: **France/tour/détour/deux/enfants** produces television which assumes that it is the subjects of the programmes who are interesting and not the makers. He argues that the interest is not provided by the producers but by those who they have chosen as their subjects — subjects who are also the very people who consume television. In response to this Berr changes tack to argue that the centre of interest in the scene we are watching is not Camille but her parents. Dray refuses to accept this, insisting that the interest is not some content that the child is presenting (it is exactly the parents who present their lives to each other and the children) but the solitude that is being discovered.

If in **Le Gai Savoir** Godard claimed that the eye must 'listen before it looks', that the dominance of sound was total, now the struggle is to make the image speak, to hear what cannot be said. If the emphasis of the Maoist period was the unity to be found in a class position, the work since **Ici et ailleurs** insists on the solitude which is the lot conferred on us by biology and reinforced by society. The *logic* that links us *all* to *reality* is a body so complicated that all it can offer is a sexuality and a death that leave us almost incommunicable islands. Sonimage's move from Paris to Grenoble and then to Rolle becomes an analogue of the necessity of confronting the solitude that cities impose but disavow. It is solitude which is one of the dominant themes in the interview **Jean-Luc** when Godard talks to the journalists from *Libération*. In place of a discourse which generalises politically from the practice of film-making, a discourse Godard adopted, however hesitantly, after '68, the journalists from *Libération* discover a discourse which only offers its particular situation and its particular relation to the image in answer to any generalisable political question. The impossible demand to start the revolution everywhere at once is replaced by the statement that communication is possible only at the moment when everywhere changes places: when the individual loses himself or herself in the effort of showing an image to someone else. If the strength of this position is its radical refusal of any dialogue which is not also an acknowledgement of solitude, its weakness is its concomitant refusal to consider the possibility of the creation of social meaning, of the grounds for communal action. The lessons of the television programmes are unequivocal: once meaning has become fully social it ceases to be communication but becomes a repetition that binds us unknowingly in our solitude.

From **Jean-Luc**

One of the few artists to whom Godard has made constant reference at almost every stage of his work is Brecht. In the interview with the journalists it is Brecht, and his solitude, that serves as one of the crucial references. But Godard either ignores, or deliberately rejects, what Brecht always held in tension with that solitude: the participation in popular and political forms. That rejection composes the **STORY** related by Albert Dray at the end of the eleventh episode of **France/tour/détour/deux/enfants.** The story starts with Dray holding up a book on May '68 by Georges Séguy, the leader of the Communist-dominated union, the CGT. He wants to explain the lie that has allowed the Communists, completely outstripped by events at the time, to claim the heritage of May '68. Dray's explanation considers silent footage of a demonstration. He emphasises how demonstrations are like television: they communicate so readily that nothing gets through. It is only when you disrupt sound and image, when one can hear nothing, that it becomes clear that something is not getting through, that is becomes possible to listen. Dray's story is unambiguous: it was the failure to break with the stereotyped political forms such as the demonstration which allowed the Communists to paralyse the novelty of May with their rhetoric. In this version of history political and aesthetic problems are virtually indistinguishable, variants of a general logic of communication. To participate in the established forms, be they political or televisual, is to lose what is specific to your experience and situation, to communicate easily at the cost of communicating nothing.

From the 11th episode of
France/tour/détour/deux/enfants

The pessimism of such a position should not be lightly dismissed, it is all too possible that we have not despaired enough, but neither should one ignore the contradictions of Dray's position, contradictions that Berr hesitantly points to in the very final scene of the progamme. If the logic of the specific is carried through to its conclusion then none of us would have anything to say to each other, no message except the constant statement of the limitations of the form that we were using. To allow that something was recuperated after May is to allow that something happened, to admit the possibility of political action, some conception of a community in which solitude can be recognised and acted upon. If the image remains there is the possibility of elaborating in sound what is there to be seen. If Dray, and perhaps Godard, simply wants an image without sound it is Godard himself who has taught us that it is always a question of the relation between the two. It is the understanding and transformation of that relation, its institutional and technological preconditions, its sexual and social implications, which is a necessary and fundamental component of any politics in the West today. It is Godard who has most fully formulated, who is most fully formulating, the terms of that relation.

From **Jean-Luc**

Colin MacCabe:

In conventional television a great deal of care is taken in the selection of people for interview and that selection is operated to find representatives of certain classes or groups. How did you select your interviewees?

Jean-Luc Godard:

We didn't select people carefully like that but it took a long time to find them. We reached them, the right people, at the right places but after a lot of time. We reached the peasant who was close at hand but after we'd tried workers in Paris, workers elsewhere, and finally then we reached the only one we could reach. But the fourth episode was completely out-dated because we didn't reach the right people.

One of the most striking features of your television is the lack of direct address.

The address is provided by the work before the shooting and after the shooting. It's in the mise-en-scène. It's to be there for that amount of time.

In your own interview, **Jean-Luc**, you talk a lot about solitude. Are your interviews a way of escaping that solitude?

It was the only way for me to speak to someone. I was unable to listen to them and not to talk. There was a man who was considered ill — who was saying silence — and that was not heavy at all. I listened. With the other ones it was very difficult because you have to talk, you have to enquire, to talk and then you look like a prosecutor — you can't avoid it. But at least I was interested.

In **Jean-Luc** the journalists from *Libération* asked you a series of questions which you seemed to regard as stupid but which, nevertheless, I want to repeat. In brief:

'Isn't the conclusion to be drawn from your television work that the whole organisation of television, the whole relation between producer and consumer is such that there can't be any real television? And the fact that, as Godard, you occupy a certain cultural position which allows you to make real television . . .?'

Well, once in your life isn't much . . . Once in my life.

But the pessimism of what you say offers very little perspective for anybody else. It's almost as if you're saying that the structures of television are so rotten that there's nothing you can do . . .

Yes. Make movies.

But isn't your position on television so pessimistic. . .?

It's industry. It's a part of myself. I think it could be better. There's too much of it, like the car industry or any other kind of industry. . .

Is there a chance of setting up a different kind of television in Mozambique?

There was a chance. A chance. It's over.

Could you explain that?

It's too far away and the chance is over because it is a country. It's difficult to say. It's like a possibility. It's rather well-defined in the beginning and then afterwards when you say it's not possible, it was not possible to go on then it becomes difficult to say. It's like a love affair. You cross a street and you change direction and then you have to separate. Why? Because one of you lived here and one of you lived over there. You could change your life but you don't change your life that easily. TV is too big. A movie is interesting because it's smaller, everyone is living in a small place. A movie is a small place

— it's a hundred people during six months. In such a place you could change but then it doesn't change in the movies, it's even more fixed there than anywhere else. Iran is changing fast, it changes faster than America. But then America can stop the war in Vietnam very much faster than Hollywood changes its system of making a picture. Hollywood has changed, the studios have changed . . . but it's technical. It's technical. It's big companies instead of small companies. It's people I don't know. It's not Jews from Hungary, it's not Selznick. Now it's a 'United'; it's a conglomerate; it's business. But still there is a camera, always just a camera and a script and you go. You go into that country if you want to write a good script. It's the only place where I think that it's easy to change if you want to. But then since I haven't succeeded in changing things I think that there must be something else. And that's the point of *The Story* — why there's no change.

In **Six Fois deux** you seem to suggest that it's the division of labour that is the original sin.

Yes, but I'm from a Protestant family. It's not a sin but a curse. Even in the last film we made a joke of the division between video and camera equipment. It's like Cain and Abel. 'What have you done with your brother?' I don't think it's the division of labour but a division of love and labour. Love is labour and you say that a woman who is having a child — you say that she is in labour. It's not division of labour but division of love and labour. There is a division between love and labour but they are two aspects of the one thing. And they say it's two different things but there's one thing with two different moments or states. There is division and they shouldn't be divided — they should be together. And if they were together it would be a multiplication not a division.

Could you explain your analysis of the sailors from *Potemkin* and communication that you put forward in **Lecons de choses**?

Potemkin is a famous movie and critics have always been interested in it but I read a book by an Englishman, a journalist I think, which really told you the facts. The Anglo-Saxons are much better at enquiring. It's not like the French or the Italians, who never enquire. In the British, the Anglo-Saxon, tradition, there is real work. They enquire about the scandals — about the facts. It was a small book which wasn't political but it was very serious. It was just interested in the facts. And it wasn't at all like Eisenstein showed it. So this book told you what the sailors had done. And I tried to analyse it in terms of communication. In fact they were communicating something. As nobody listened they had to go back to the cruiser and try to find a port and then it was all over. But that was the real story of Potemkin. It was not what the Russians say in their books or in their schools. Those were the facts. That's what happened. In a

sense they were making a movie when they were parading. They wanted to be heard by some others . . .

It's almost as if you are saying that in order to communicate you must find new forms.

Yes, they were using a new form of communication and that's why it was so crucial and so unfulfilled in a sense at the time. It was in 1905 and it was only fulfilled twenty years later. In the West, in our time, it takes thirty years, more or less, for an image to appear and to be fulfilled. It's what they call the age of reason — to become an adult it takes thirty years and it's the same for an image ★ .

★ The age of reason is reached at the age of thirty in French.

You almost seem to be saying that if there's a powerful enough feeling it will be communicated. It will find a new form and it will communicate itself.

No. I'm trying to say, in opposition to the history defined by the standard texts, that they were not revolting, that they were not trying to kill the czar. They were not making a revolution, they didn't think of themselves as revolutionaries. They were communicating. They were trying to put something into something else. Which may be the real method for revolution but they did not think of themselves in the way they were represented later. It was something different.

Are you saying that at the moment the sailors became an image they ceased to communicate?

Well, I don't know . . . But this was the real story, which I like because it's been forgotten, like the real story of the death of Che Guevara.

Which is what?

When he said: 'Let's make three or four Vietnams', he didn't realise that because they were fighting if you make three Vietnams you make three USAs as well.

All through the book I'm concerned to explain the value of your work on sound and image and to write against that organisation of sound and image which puts you in the position of the tourist. But I'm also conscious that very often what I want to see is not a television programme like **Six Fois deux** or **France/tour/detour/deux/enfants** but *Dallas* or *Blake's Seven*.

Yes. It's like that for me too.

But then my problem — and it may well be mine and not yours — is:

How do you find a way of explaining what's good about your work without taking up a very moralistic discourse which condemns more traditional and conventional work as bad?

No, I'm not saying . . . I'm trying to do what you want to do. You want to record — the machine's recording — then, good, we're recording it. That's why I like technicians or doctors. They say 'Well, if we took the magnetic out of the tape then it wouldn't be any good.' Then you can speak about something — that's what I call speaking. And sometimes you can't speak about a solid object, you speak about immaterial objects but if you're really speaking then that's material as well. But then there's another way of speaking about most of these things and I just don't understand what people are speaking about. It's all right maybe with football fans because I know what they're speaking about so I can relax. There's a third term. But most of the time people are speaking the other way and there's no communication. You must have an angle to understand. And you don't have to speak — there's play, playing sport. There's no speaking but you understand because you are viewing direct communication. You can't return a tennis ball and speak to your partner. You don't have the physical strength to do both together.

If I said the trouble with your television programmes is that they're boring . . .

No, the trouble is that you can't see their exhilaration — the exhilaration in all my work. They don't suit the time that you're looking at them because you're obliged to live in this society. If you're too much alone, you become exhilarated. You claim that what you do is good but it's too good . . . like the other stuff is too bad. I don't want to oblige people to make pictures my way but they shouldn't oblige me to make a picture their way. Up to now it's been me who's been more under the obligation to make it their way. It should be more just . . . But of course I don't think it's boring. If you look at them all at once then they're boring but you shouldn't see them like that. But then you can't see them the way they should be seen. But if you catch ten minutes out of the hour you watch — that's very rich. And it shouldn't be done in such a concentrated way — I should do it every month. But also you should remember that they're made for people in my country, not for people outside. I don't pretend to interest people from outside. Or only perhaps with movies. And then only once every four years or something like that . . . not every time.

. . . If I was master of the world there would only be one picture and I would oblige every country to make it each year in turn. The

same actors, the same story would go out from a different country each year.

I wasn't saying that I found them boring. I was talking of people who do find them boring and the problem of convincing them . . .

But I'm not trying to convince people. But people believe that when you use a certain way of thinking that you are trying to convince them and it's hard to explain that you're not. In *France/tour/détour/ deux/enfants* **what I say is that if you look you can see that it's not good but how can you escape it? And it looks as though we're trying to have the last word. But we're trying to have the first word.**

So it's not a question of convincing people but of having the first word?

Yes. But in a way no matter what I do . . . if I am polite they say I'm sarcastic, if I'm angry they say I'm insincere. You do your thing . . . You try to be strong but in a smoother way.

But what are you trying to do?

I need to talk and to show me talking, to show and to show me showing. And when I've done that I need to talk about it technically and philosophically. I need to have a philosophical talk on the technical aspect and a technical talk on the philosophical aspect. It's like Socrates, who was just trying to talk to people. And then everybody got so completely angry that they obliged him to commit suicide. He was just trying to say 'Are you sure?' — which was his way. They should at least have talked to him for a bit instead of doing what they did. But it was too strong. I don't know why. All he was saying to people was 'Are you sure you're right?' 'Is your hair well-cut?' 'Do you think that's the right way to cut it?' And they said 'Oh, Socrates. What are you doing? What are you driving at?' And he said 'I'm not driving at anything but are you sure your hair is right?'

Godard directing the *Hornuss* sequence
from **Sauve qui peut** (see pp.43-44).
Production stills from this sequence
are shown overleaf.

161

From **Sauve qui peut**

Love comes from work

Work comes from love

At the same time that they exchanged news concerning
themselves (this would at last be the occasion to
get a divorce, Reno being so close to Las Vegas),
they spoke of Frankie's project .

Roberto thinks that Frankie has the desire to make
a pot of dough and a new name for himself. But he's
taking a big risk too , if he says anything at all
about the Mafia and show business.

Diana agrees , to a certain extent, but also
thinks that Frankie wants to do something that's
never been done , and she believes in Frankie's
sincerity.

28

There's a story between us.As with other people,
the story comes out of <u>him</u> and goes back home
into <u>her</u> . And there,in<u>side</u>,you loose track.
And t<u>hen</u> the story reappears,a child is born,
and you find that outside,in the outer world.
And there,you can see again the <u>story</u>.

Il y a une histoire entre nous.Comme pour tout
le monde,l'histoire sort de chez lui et rentre
chez elle . Et là , à l'intérieur ,on perd sa
trace.Et puis elle ressort,un enfant est né,
et on trouve ça dehors , à l'extérieur.Et là,
on voit de nouveau l'histoire.

Alone in her room , Diana , after switching off
and on the light several times ,finally calls a
number she finds in a magazine about Las Vegas,
and asks ,if instead of a woman ,the agency
could send her a man.

No problem.They call back and say it being so
late ,all that's left is a Mexican,is it all
the same to her.Diana says yes.

3.

After a while , Roberto pays ,gets up , and look at Diana before leaving.

He goes towards her.He says that Frankie asked him to tell Diana that he couldn't come.They've all got a date the next morning to decide about the rest of the shooting in Las Vegas(when asked (later)what by Diana , Roberto said something about Howard Hughes and the hidden years).

Diana asks him why he didn't say something right away . Roberto answers that she didn't ask him anything either. She immediately insults him obscenely. He sits down next to her .He says well it looks like nothing's changed.

23

SCOUNDREL TIME

The House Committee
on Un-American
Activities, 1948:
Chairman
J. Parnell Thomas
second from left,
Representative
Richard M. Nixon

"I CANNOT AND WILL NOT
CUT MY CONSCIENCE TO FIT
THIS YEAR'S FASHIONS."

55' - 60'

Check list of Godard's work in Film and Television

There is a complete filmography of Godard's pre-1968 film in Roud (1970).

When there are two English-language titles, the first is British, the second American.

Films made by Jean-Luc Godard

1954

Opération béton
20 minutes
Production: Actua Film (Geneva)
Photography: Adrien Porchet
Editing: Godard

1955

Une Femme coquette
10 minutes 16 mm
Production: Jean-Luc Godard (Geneva)
Script: Hans Lucas (Jean-Luc Godard), based on Maupassant's story *Le Signe*
Photography: Hans Lucas
Editing: Hans Lucas

1957

Tous les garçons s'appellent Patrick ou Charlotte et Véronique (All Boys Are Called Patrick)
21 minutes
Production: Les Films de la Pléïade (Paris)
Script: Eric Rohmer
Photography: Michel Latouche
Editing: Cécile Decugis

1958

Charlotte et son Jules
20 minutes
Production: Les Films de la Pléïade
Script: Godard
Photography: Michel Latouche
Editing: Cécile Decugis

Une Histoire d'eau
18 minutes
Production: Les Films de la Pléïade (Pierre Braunberger)
Co-Director: François Truffaut
Script: Truffaut
Photography: Michel Latouche
Editing: Godard

1959

A bout de souffle (Breathless)
89 minutes
Production: Georges de Beauregard, Sociéte Nouvelle de Cinéma (Paris)
Script: Godard based on an idea by Francois Truffaut
Photography: Raoul Coutard
Editing: Cécile Decugis, Lila Herman

169

1960

Le Petit Soldat
(The Little Soldier)
87 minutes
Production: Georges de Beauregard, SNC
(Paris)
Photography: Raoul Coutard, Michel
Latouche
Editing: Agnès Guillemot, Nadine
Marquand, Lila Herman

1961

Une Femme est une femme
(A Woman Is a Woman)
84 minutes
Production: Rome-Paris Films (Paris)
Script: Godard, based on an idea by
Geneviève Cluny
Photography: Raoul Coutard
Editing: Agnés Guillemot, Lila Herman

La Paresse
(sketch in *Les Sept Péchés capitaux*)
Production: Films Gibé, Franco-London
Films (Paris), Titanus (Rome)
Photography: Henri Decaë, Jean-Paul
Schwartz
Editing: Jacques Gaillard

1962

Vivre sa vie
(It's My Life; My life to Live)
85 minutes
Production: Les Films de la Pléïade (Paris)
Script: Godard, documentation from *Où en
est la prostitution?,* by Judge Marcel
Sacotte
Photography: Raoul Coutard, Claude
Beausoleil, Charles Bitsch
Editing: Agnès Guillemot, Lila Lakshmanan

Le Nouveau Monde
(sketch in *RoGoPaG*)
20 minutes
Production: Lyre Film
(Paris), Arco Film Cineriz (Rome)
Photography: Jean Rabier
Editing: Agnès Guillemot, Lila Lakshmanan

1962-63

Les Carabiniers
(The Soldiers; The Riflemen)
80 minutes
Production: Rome-Paris Films (Paris),
Laetitia (Rome)
Script: Jean-Luc Godard, Jean Gruault,
Roberto Rossellini, from Jacques Audi-
berti's French adaption of Benjamino
Joppolo's play, *I Carabinieri*
Photography: Raoul Coutard, Claude
Beausoleil
Editing: Agnès Guillemot, Lila Lakshmanan

1963

Le Grand Escroc
(sketch in *Les Plus Belles Escroqueries
du monde*)
25 minutes
Production: Ulysse Productions (Paris),
Primex Films (Marseille), Vides (Rome),
Toho (Tokyo), Caesar Film (Amsterdam)
Photography: Raoul Coutard
Editing: Agnès Guillemot, Lila Lakshmanan

Le Mépris (Contempt)
105 minutes
Production: Rome-Paris Films, Films
Concordia (Paris), Compagnia
Cinematografica Champion (Rome)
Script: Godard, based on Alberto Moravia's
novel, *Il Disprezzo*
Photography: Raoul Coutard
Editing: Agnès Guillemot, Lila Lakshmanan

Montparnasse-Levallois
(sketch in *Paris vu par . . .*)
18 minutes 16mm, later blown up to 35mm
Production: Les Films du Losange (Paris),
Barbet Schroeder
Script: Godard
Photography: Albert Maysles
Editing: Jacqueline Raynal

1964

Bande à part
(Band of Outsiders;
The Outsiders)
95 minutes
Production: Anouchka Films, Orsay Films
(Paris)
Script: Godard, based on the novel *Fool's
Gold* (*Pigeon Vole*) by Dolores Hitchens
Photography: Raoul Coutard, Georges
Liron
Editing: Agnès Guillemot, Francoise Collin

**Une Femme mariée
(A Married Woman;
The Married Woman)**
95 minutes
Production: Anouchka Films, Orsay Films
(Paris)
Script: Godard
Photography: Raoul Coutard
Editing: Agnès Guillemot, Françoise Collin

1965

**Alphaville ou Une étrange aventure de
Lemmy Caution**
98 minutes
Production: Chaumiane Production
(Paris), Filmstudio (Rome)
Photography: Raoul Coutard, Georges
Liron
Editing: Agnès Guillemot

Pierrot le fou
112 minutes
Production: Rome-Paris Films
(Paris), Dino de Laurentiis,
Cinematografia (Rome)
Script: Godard, based on Lionel White's
novel *Obsession*
Photography: Raoul Coutard, Georges
Liron
Editing: Françoise Collin

1966

**Masculin/Féminin
(Masculine/Feminine)**
110 minutes
Production: Anouchka Films, Argos Films,
(Paris) Svensk Filmindustri, Sandrews
(Stockholm)
Script: Godard, loosely based on two
stories by Guy de Maupassant, *La Femme
de Paul* and *Le Signe*
Photography: Willy Kurant
Editing: Agnès Guillemot

Made in USA
90 minutes
Production: Rome-Paris Films, Anouchka
Films, SEPIC (Paris)
Script: Godard, based on Richard Stark's
novel *Rien dans le coffre*
Photography: Raoul Coutard, Georges
Liron
Editing: Agnès Guillemot

**Deux ou trois choses que je sais d'elle
(Two or Three Things I know about her)**
90 minutes
Production: Anouchka Films, Argos Films,
Les Films du Carosse, Parc Film (Paris)
Script: Godard, suggested by two articles of
Catherine Vimenet, 'La Prostitution dans
les grands ensembles', *Le Nouvel
observateur,* 29 March and 10 May 1966
Photography: Raoul Coutard, Georges
Liron
Editing: Françoise Collin, Chantal Delattre

Anticipation ou L'an 2000
(sketch in *Le Plus vieux métier du monde*)
Production: Francoriz Films, Films Gibé,
(Paris), Rialto Films (Berlin), Rizzoli Films
(Rome)
Photography: Pierre Lhomme
Editing: Agnès Guillemot

1967

La Chinoise, ou plutôt à la chinoise
90 minutes
Production: Anouchka Films, Les
Productions de la Guéville, Athos Films,
Parc Films, Simar Films (Paris)
Photography: Raoul Coutard, Georges
Liron
Editing: Agnès Guillemot, Delphine
Desfons

Caméra-Oeil
(episode in *Loin du Viêt-nam*)
115 minutes (entire film)
Production: SLON (Paris)
Uncredited supervisory editor: Chris
Marker

L'Amour
(original title: **Andante e ritorno dei
figli prodighi**)
(sketch in *Amore e Rabbia*;
original title: *Vangelo 70*)
26 minutes
Production: Castoro Films (Rome),
Anouchka Films (Paris)
Photography: Alain Levent
Editing: Agnès Guillemot

Weekend
95 minutes
Production: Comacico Lira Films, Films Copernic (France), Ascot Cineraïd (Rome),

Photography: Raoul Coutard
Editing: Agnès Guillemot

1968

Le Gai Savoir
95 minutes
Production: Originally ORTF (French Radio and Television); later Anouchka Films (Paris), Bavaria Atelier (Munich)
Photography: Jean Leclerc
Editing: Germaine Cohen

Un Film comme les autres
(A Movie Like the Others)
Time estimates run from 100 to 120 minutes. 16 mm
Filmed by the Dziga-Vertov group, with shots by the 'Etats Généraux du Cinéma' interspersed

One Plus One
(producer's title:
Sympathy for the Devil)
99 minutes
Production: Cupid Productions, Inc.
Photography: Tony Richmond, Colin Corby
Editing: Ken Rowless, Agnès Guillemot

1968-69

One American Movie/1 A.M.
Definitively abandoned by Godard in March 1970. 16 mm. Footage from this film, plus footage on the film being made, were put together by the producer, D.A. Pennebaker, and entitled *One P.M.* This film was released in 1971.
82 minutes
Production: Leacock-Pennebaker, Inc.
Script: Pennebaker, Godard
Photography: Richard Leacock, D.A. Pennebaker
Editing: D.A. Pennebaker

Films made by
the Dziga-Vertov Group

From the establishment of the Dziga-Vertov group, Godard and his collaborators have done their own editing, unless otherwise stated.

1969

British Sounds (See You at Mao)
52 minutes. 16 mm
Production : Kestrel Productions (for London Weekend Television)
Photography: Charles Stewart
Editing: Elizabeth Kozmian

Pravda
76 minutes. 16 mm
Production: Centre Européen Cinéma Radio Télévision

1970

Vento dell'est (Vent d'est; East Wind)
100 minutes. 16 mm (also 35 mm blow-up)
Production: CCC (Berlin), Poli Film (Rome), Anouchka Films (Paris)
Script: Daniel Cohn-Bendit
Photography: Mario Vulpiano

Lotte in Italia
(Luttes en Italie; Struggle in Italy)
76 minutes. 16 mm
Production: Cosmoseion (Rome), for the RAI (Italian Radio & Television)

Vladimir et Rosa (Vladimir and Rosa)
106 minutes. 16 mm
Production: Grove Press, Evergreen Films (USA), German Television

Jusqu'à la victoire (Till Victory)
16 mm
This film remained unfinished. Much of the footage was used in *Ici et ailleurs*

Films made by Jean-Luc Godard and Jean-Pierre Gorin

1972

Tout va bien
95 minutes
Script: Godard and Gorin
Photography: Armand Marco
Editing: Kenout Peltier

Letter to Jane
52 minutes. 16 mm
Production: Jean-Luc Godard and
Jean-Pierre Gorin

Films made by Jean-Luc Godard and Anne-Marie Miéville

1974

Ici et ailleurs
55 minutes. 16 mm
Production: Institut National de l'Audiovisuel (Paris) and Sonimage (Grenoble)

1975

Numéro deux
88 minutes
Production: Sonimage (Grenoble), Bela
Productions, SNC (Paris)
Video Engineer: Gérard Teissèdre
Technical Collaborators: Milka Assaf,
Gérard Martin

1976

Comment ça va
78 minutes
Production: Sonimage (Grenoble), Institut
National de l'Audiovisuel, Bela
Productions, SNC (Paris)
Photography: William Lubtchansky

1980

Sauve qui peut (La Vie)/(Slow Motion)
90 minutes (approx.)
Production: Sonimage (Rolle), Sara Films
(Geneva), MK2, Saga Productions (Paris)
Photography: Renato Berta, William
Lubtchansky

Television produced and directed by Jean-Luc Godard and Anne-Marie Miéville

1976

Sur et sous la communication (Six Fois deux)
600 minutes (six programmes, each composed
of two fifty-minute sections)
Production: Institut National de
l'Audiovisuel (Paris), and Sonimage
(Grenoble)
Video Engineer: Gerard Teissèdre
Photography: William Lubtchansky,
Dominique Chapuis

1978

France/tour/détour/deux/enfants
Production: Institut National de
l'Audiovisuel (Paris) and Sonimage (Rolle)
360 minutes (twelve half-hour programmes)
Script: Loosely based on 'La Tour de la
France par deux enfants' by G.Bruno
Video: P.Bingelli
Photography: W.Lubtchansky, D.Chapuis,
P.Rony

Select Bibliography

The British Film Institute's *Book Library Bibliography no.19* (1976) is the most complete guide to writings on and by Godard. There is also a full bibliography in Brown (1972).

I would like to take this opportunity to thank Andi Engel of Artificial Eye for letting me consult his large collection of newspaper and magazine cuttings on Godard.

Althusser, Louis (1971)
'Ideology and Ideological State Apparatuses: Notes towards an investigation' in *Lenin and Philosophy and other essays.* (London: New Left Books)

L'Avant-Scène du Cinéma July/September 1976, nos.171-172

Brown, Royal S. (1972) *editor*
Focus on Godard.
(Englewood Cliffs, N.J.: Prentice Hall)

Coutard, Raoul (1965)
'Light of Day',
Sight and Sound, Winter 1965/6 vol.35, no.1. pp.9-11

Evans, Harold (1978)
Pictures on the Page
(London: Heinemann)

Godard, Jean-Luc (1972)
Godard on Godard, edited and translated by Tom Milne
(London: Secker and Warburg)

Godard, Jean-Luc (1979) *editor*
Cahiers du Cinéma, no.300

Godard, Jean-Luc (1980)
Introduction à une véritable histoire du cinéma, vol.1
Paris: Editions Albatross.
Two further volumes forthcoming.

Harvey, Sylvia (1978) 'Woman's place: the absent family of film noir' in *Women in Film noir* edited by E. Ann Kaplan. (London: British Film Institute)

Heath, Stephen and Skirrow, Gillian (1977)
'Television: a world in action'
Screen vol.18, no.2, pp.7-77

MacBean, James Roy (1975)
Film and Revolution
(Bloomington, London: Indiana University Press)

Roud, Richard (1970)
Jean-Luc Godard, 2nd edition.
(London: Secker and Warburg)

Williams, Raymond (1974)
Television: Technology and Cultural Form
(London: Fontana)

British Film Institute Cinema Series

Edited by Ed Buscombe

The British Film Institute Cinema Series opens up a new area of cinema publishing with books that will appeal to people who are already interested in the cinema but want to know more, written in an accessible style by authors who have some authority in their field. The authors write about areas of the cinema where there is substantial popular interest, but as yet little serious writing, or they bring together for a wider audience some of the important ideas which have been developed in film studies in recent years.

Published:

Colin MacCabe: **Godard: Images, Sounds, Politics**

Forthcoming:

Richard Dyer: **The Stars**

Thomas Elsaesser: **New German Cinema**

Jane Feuer: **The Hollywood Musical**

Angela Martin: **Women and Film**

Steve Neale: **Cinema and Technology**

Christopher Williams: **Film and Marxism**